LIFE BEHIND THE BADGE

by
D. W. Driver

PublishAmerica
Baltimore

First printing

ISBN: 1-59129-423-1
PUBLISHED BY PUBLISHAMERICA BOOK PUBLISHERS
www.publishamerica.com
Baltimore

Printed in the United States of America

~ *DEDICATION* ~

To the loves of my life Kelli & Kristen.
To Bob Sr. who was always there even when he wasn't.
To Shirley Deane & Vic "The Australian Connection"— thanks,
Mom. I love you.
To Bill Allen, without whose help this book would not
be a reality.
And especially to Bob Jr., truly my best man.

In Memoriam:
To the fallen badges of
September 11, 2001

Contents

Introduction   7

Chapter One   The Good Guys   9
Chapter Two   The Law   15
Chapter Three   The Drunk Driver   28
Chapter Four   Juvenile Crime   44
Chapter Five   A Cop's Home Life   54
Chapter Six   The White Collar World   61
Chapter Seven   Shift Change   69
Chapter Eight   The Pursuit   83
Chapter Nine   Out On Patrol   92
Chapter Ten   Driving A Desk   103
Chapter Eleven   You Get Promoted   110
Chapter Twelve   A Cop's Day Off   115
Chapter Thirteen   From A Recruit's Eyes   121
Chapter Fourteen   The Death Penalty   133
Chapter Fifteen   To Bury A Cop   134
Chapter Sixteen   Some Final Thoughts   139

General Request To The American Public   143
A Short Biography of the Author   145
Accomplishments   147

INTRODUCTION

Books and movies about cops have been done to death. Why? Because the action sells tickets and the good guys always crush evil and save the frail. That's beautiful in the theater. What you're about to experience is *life*. Everything you are about to read is real. I won't win every time. The bad guy won't always rot in jail. And there won't be any parades held in my honor before I drive my city car home to a quaint little ranch in a blissful meadow in Never-never Land.

What you are going to experience is the "actual" life of a cop, and a successful one by "cop" standards. But if you break down the cost of my living "behind the badge" in terms of dollars and cents versus quiet evenings at home you will begin to understand why we aren't in it for the money. It means more than that.

I always knew I'd be a cop. It didn't matter that as a child I was always the smallest one in the class. To jump ahead a chapter, I was 104 pounds when I first put on a uniform. In those days, all you had to do was show up and say "I want the job," they said okay and you were a cop (if you knew somebody). I wish I had realized then that our communities, which demand so much in terms of professionalism, would spend so little on training and support. They have no idea that is really involved in fulfilling their expectations.

There is a very obvious reason why being a cop never grows old. Simply, because "copping" never stays the same. What was common practice in the fifties is archaic in the eighties. What was pro-active enforcement in the seventies is civil abuse in the nineties. If you don't say please, you get complained on and you visit the carpet. If the handcuffs are too tight, you get sued, the department says, "We trained him better than that," and you really understand the feeling of walking that thin blue line alone.

D. W. Driver

Please think of this, above all that you will read, as the basis of every cop's reality:
You give me a car to drive, but I'd better not wreck it.
You give me a gun to save lives, but I'd better not shoot it.
Above all, you give me a badge to wear, but god knows I'd better not tarnish it.
I'm not allowed to err, but I must be human.
What follows, is living behind, and for, *the badge*.

CHAPTER ONE
The Good Guys

I've always admired the law enforcement profession. As a child I would watch in excited amazement, as our car would drive by a traffic stop on a hot Texas night. Squinting through the flashing red and blue lights as my parents drove slowly by. I wanted more than anything to be wearing that uniform. To me, all cops were good, all cops cared and all cops were invincible.

Little in my life has caused me more pain than the first time I heard about a bad cop. I didn't want to believe it. They must have made a mistake, I told myself. It's not possible that a cop would *steal*. A cop *can't* sell drugs. No *way* could a police officer hit his wife, abuse his child. It didn't fit my version of reality.

In hindsight, I now realize that the lowest base of that pedestal I placed every cop on was too high for the best of us to ever reach. But even now, every day I put on a uniform I strive to reach that pinnacle. I pray that on the day I stop climbing toward it that I will have the wisdom to know that it's time to leave that uniform in the closet. When the hunger for perfection that every cop feels as a rookie, eager to clean up the streets, begins to waiver, it's time to get help.

I mentioned my physical stature in the Introduction. When I was finally old enough to play cop I was 104 pounds and barely tall enough to get on most of the rides at Disneyland. Mine was truly an uphill battle. Back then I didn't realize how many times that "short-coming" would benefit me as a police officer.

I went against even my own preconceived notions of being a cop. I thought you had to be huge. When I was growing up, if you had an encounter with an officer, you expected this hopefully compassionate six-foot *Terminator* to awe you with his mere presence. Now, in the middle of my second decade of wearing the uniform, I've ballooned to the impressive stature of a high school sophomore hoping to make the chess team. If I've heard "Barney Fife" once I've heard it a million times.

Upsetting? Sure, at first. Remember, I lived to be a cop, respected the profession more than life itself and here I was bringing disrespect to that which I so cherished. Fortunately, my sense of humor far exceeded my physical stature. Eventually my "weakness" became a strength. Aided by a fair "Fife" impersonation I learned that I could put people at ease, sometimes actually making friends where other cops might intimidate and escalate a situation by their appearance. To this day, none can stump me on Mayberry trivia (I still carry a bullet in my pocket).

Law enforcement has changed since I was a kid. Small men, tall women, all races, you name it. Though it initially met with resistance, we need variety, desperately. Not just in law enforcement, but in life.

I'm no philosopher, I don't have a doctorate in social sciences nor do I claim to have any special expertise in human relations. This observation is personal, very personal. I've seen the deteriorating racial relations that are eroding our nation—a readiness of people to attack each other, verbally and physically, based on the thin outer layer of their skin.

Before you finish this book, you'll hear about the crimes, the death, and the gore, all in detail. But of all the problems in our society I feel this is the most insidious. If the ongoing trend of racial hatred continues, we–police and citizens alike–will eventually drown in our own ignorance.

I remember, while working as a campus police officer in Tahlequah, Oklahoma, that the Department of Justice alerted school campuses of the expected potential for continuing and increasing race/hate crimes.

A half a dozen years earlier, I'd lived in the bottom floor of the sports dorm. Ordinarily, this area was reserved for the basketball team. Not only did I greet my co-residents at about knee level, but the pigment of our skins was certainly in contrast. Never have I had the pleasure of having better friends. Fortunately, in 1981, we were allowed to be friends. We were blessedly ignorant of the future that was just then beginning to make its way out of the large cities, a disease unknown to many of us but well on it's way.

A fire can spread only so far before no amount of water in the world can extinguish it. As police officers, we have the unique opportunity to be the social firefighters of our respective communities.

One bad cop makes all the media. It owns the headlines, sells newspapers and blankets our TV screens. When our children see this every night, hear it on the school grounds, and even the earliest years of innocence are alienated how can we expect this trend to go away? Change must be immediate and sincere.

Let's shift gears and get back to the positive aspects of being a law enforcement professional. We have the opportunity to help people every single day, and that's not just limited to our on-duty life. We still help kids cross the street, some still carry groceries for the elderly and saving a life continues to be the highlight of a career. Sure, the adrenaline-packed excitement of a foot pursuit ending with the bad guy in handcuffs is a true thrill that my words certainly cannot do justice. Realistically though, a very small percentage of our enforcement duties are so typical of the commercialized excitement that most watch at home or in the theaters.

The new trend in law enforcement today is community oriented policing. A successful police officer now must excel in public relations. You must be authoritative without being intimidating and you must overpower without being forceful. Now that's a tough job. How many reading this book could be spit on one night and be willing to do everything in your power to protect that very person from harm the next morning?

Though I am supportive of preventative programs to educate, we cannot hide behind these ideas, hoping that the present issues in need of immediate attention will fade away. Nothing is more frustrating than seeing millions and millions of dollars spent on prevention when we have police officers so poorly equipped that performing their jobs safely and effectively is impossible.

To this day, we have law enforcement personnel that cannot do their jobs. Not because of apathy, but because of the almighty dollar. Many must supply their own uniforms but we expect nothing short of immaculate appearance.

Many either cannot financially afford a degree in higher learning or, more commonly, do not have the time to return to school. Yet, they are expected to have the wisdom of a Rhode's scholar when asked a question or asked to render an immediate decision.

We operate vehicles that are often worn out and even unsafe, yet again, our response must be immediate. You can't please everyone and I have almost lost my sanity trying.

In spite of this, it is vital for every present or future public servant reading this book to try at every opportunity to make our profession shine in the eyes of the public we serve. This attitude benefits both the community/citizens and your professional career.

So many young police officers limit themselves, unknowingly, as the result of "veteran" officers displaying an apathetic disposition. The old credo of "the more you do, the greater your chance of a complaint" drains the blood from potential law enforcement icons. It is of paramount importance that new recruits be nourished with support and a helping hand up when they fall, not kicked for having tried and failed.

This brings me to probably the most sensitive issue I can relate to the future success of law enforcement. We must have the support of two entities if we, as law enforcement officers are to succeed. Without the support of your agency you will fail to be motivated and without the support of the community you will fail to be pro-active.

Nothing, but nothing, is more sickening to me than to see an officer that acts like the agency he/she works for owes them a living just for putting on a uniform. It is no longer a thrill to serve but an inconvenience to be summoned. Desire and motivation are replaced with "let a new hire handle it," or, and I really hate this one, "I've got seniority." Now we not only have an officer that isn't pulling his/her weight but their actions, as stated above, have instilled the utmost of negative reinforcement in those that still do. Compound this with the lack of opportunity for someone waiting in the wings for their chance to serve the community and everybody loses.

Obviously, the best strategy is to see the potential for a problem, counter with a solution before it becomes a problem and maintain support for your troops.

Veteran officers need to be recognized and rewarded for the years of their lives they have dedicated to public service, however, to allow all that they have worked for to dissolve–to burnout, if you will, is an unacceptable and tragic loss.

In a perfect world, we all work as hard as we can, with devotion and loyalty not requiring a thought process. If we can instill in the veterans the reason they first put on a uniform, and return to them those values that they possessed when they first applied, we all win.

What an eye-opener it would be for all experienced, veteran police officers to see a videotape of their initial interview. The, "just give me a chance and you won't regret it," or "I'll give you 110%," might be just the ticket to prompt a rebirth of values.

It takes a special person to be cop, a special person to want to be a cop and, of much more difficulty, a very special person to be successful as a cop.

To be a successful police officer is the alpha and omega of employment careers. I know of no profession that is so easy to do at one point and so very trying the next. Ironically, if you work your entire shift without a call, you bring home the same money as when you extricate the lifeless body of an infant from a mangled piece of machinery.

An hour later, with the death of a small child encompassing your every thought, you then respond to another call requesting your services. They, the public you have sworn to serve and protect, neither understand what you have just done, the vividly grotesque memories you never allow to leave your spirit, nor will they understand why "the nice officer" wasn't as friendly as he's supposed to be. Many will think his/her lack of compassion and abruptness means they are "badge heavy."

I challenge anyone with the audacity to second guess the police to live just one day inside the vest of a police officer–to be thought of as a mindless Neanderthal who lives on coffee and donuts (although I do average about twenty-five cups on any given shift). To have no concept of what I have to go through and yet have the audacity to tell me how to do my job–*that* is frustrating.

If you have the courage to try, if you'd be willing to attempt to do that which I must do every day, if you are willing to put yourself in the position of making life or death decisions in a heartbeat then I'll be glad to sit in the passenger seat and second guess *your* actions. Remember, you don't have the option of seating a committee to plan your next move. Your decisions must be immediate and, more importantly, you must be right every time. To make an improper decision means you are "on the carpet" at the department and a zillion attorneys would drool at the prospect of telling a jury what a horrible person you are and what terrible injustices you have perpetrated against their "oh so innocent" client. But I am getting ahead of myself. We'll save lawyers for the next chapter. Things don't always work out. If it was an easy job, and paid well enough, we'd all be cops. It's not easy though, it doesn't pay well and not everyone that could be a cop would want to be a cop.

A fact about the financial side of being a police officer. When I first became a policeman I brought home one check a month, the take home amount being less than $550.00. I made more money working a second forty-hour a week job as a convenience store attendant.

Recently, a law enforcement officer made the headlines here because he applied for, and received, food stamps. This is a veteran police officer, folks, working for a large agency. My take home money listed above was in 1985; the officer with the food stamps was in 1996. That's not a great leap nor much of a motivator for those involved in, or wishing to become, a part of the law enforcement teams.

You don't become a cop for the financial stability but you must be realistic, as well. Your family has to eat, rent must be paid and clothes must be bought.

I recall one day, when looking under the seat of my wife's car, we found about $12.00 in quarters. We had to use pay washing machines for years and that washing machine money collected under the seats while loading and unloading the clothes. You would have thought we struck oil. It was really that bad in the beginning.

But it was the price I was ready and willing to pay to be one of "The Good Guys."

14

CHAPTER TWO
The Law

Let me explain my personal feelings about lawyers. Just as it's unfair for lawyers to categorize the police, it is equally unfair for the police to stereotype every barrister of justice. If I had the desire to write a book that encompassed all the lawyer jokes I've heard through the years, I'd need a manuscript the size of a full set of the *Encyclopedia Britannica.*

It's a common theme, at least in law enforcement, that you become an assistant district attorney to better our lives and you become a defense attorney to better your bank account. A truly sad day in the life of a lawyer, in my opinion, is when the almighty dollar rules the values of a lawyer's heart. Just as I hope every cop wants to serve the public, I would equally wish for the motivation of years of law school, climaxed by successfully passing the bar, result in a lawyer fulfilling his/her desire to "serve justice."

There is a common theme that should co-exist with both attorneys and law enforcement officers for as long as both professions are in demand. The Fourth Amendment of the United States Constitution guarantees "...the right of the people to be secure in their persons, houses, papers and effects..." The police, in response to almost every call for service, are trying to protect at least one of those basic constitutional rights. My wish would be that all legal professionals would harbor similar ideals while wearing their $1,200 suits.

Many times I have contemplated pursuing a law degree, not to change professions, but to improve on the one that I have chosen. I know of no greater feeling than when, in a court of law, the defense not only fails in their desire to destroy my testimony with my uncontrollable emotion but they, in turn, become emotional at my failure to "explode on the stand." The epitome of sadness is, in every courtroom in the nation, that the best salesman wins the battle.

As police officers, we are limited to expressing the facts as known and the defense "wins" by allowing their salesmanship to set the guilty free. Yes, I would be sickened by the thought of an innocent person sent to jail. More common, however, is the reality of the guilty going free, and I see or hear of it every, single day.

I have never lost a municipal court case, and I take considerable pride in that fact. The main reason, in my opinion, is that I've never written a ticket or arrested a person that didn't deserve my effecting that response. Short of school zones, I've not written a speeding ticket for at least thirteen miles an hour over the posted limit nor have I arrested a person that didn't violate a law, code or statute that warranted an arrest.

Far beyond the legal reasons listed, when given the opportunity, I treat every violator with much more respect than is, and I hate to say it, necessary. If you're too friendly, the innocent may take your actions as being forward and, of vital importance to officer safety, your niceness can be a signal to "true criminals" as a sign of weakness.

The first, of two, cases I ever lost in a district court of law was an intoxicated driver that was, admittedly, in possession of cocaine. The violation was the result of his actions while driving, specifically, driving left of the centerline (weaving). I used the same statute that had been used forever, on a "cheat sheet" that listed district traffic charges, that all members of my department utilized.

The attorney for the defense determined that the statute, taken in context from Oklahoma State Statutes, was referring to driving left of the center median of a divided highway, not a typical street. The judge agreed that, as a result of the technicality as written, the stop was ruled invalid based on the statute written on the original citation and the stop was, therefore, not valid.

It mattered not that a suspect was intoxicated, possessed narcotics and committed a traffic offense, all at his own admission. Justice is apparently blind, and sometimes deaf and dumb as well. But, that's the system.

Allow me to tell you of a scam that involved a woman (and that's being very kind) who was a career criminal in all aspects yet could not have thought up this one on her own. She had more tattoos than Charles Manson, never wore a bra, had a ring on every finger (and anything else that could be pierced) and her daily dialogue would make a Satanist blush. What I'm about to tell you happens commonly, but usually on a much smaller scale.

This "lady" will go to a pharmacy, obtain a couple of very

expensive medicinal items, a couple hundred dollars worth, pay for them in cash, then leave.

She'll wait for about an hour (probably doing a little smack to pass the time) and then re-enter the same store. She presents the items to the same clerk, says she bought the wrong stuff (probably for dear old mom who's too sick to buy it herself) and pleasantly requests a refund.

If the clerk asks for a receipt, our clever crook makes an excuse, such as "must have lost it," or "it must have flown out of the bag," and, since the clerk saw her pay cash just a short time ago, she gets the cash refund.

Okay, some might say, she paid cash for the items, brought the items back and got the cash back. What's the problem?

I'll tell you–she still has the receipt. Now, she goes to another store and shoplifts the same items (and that's real easy to do), from a different area but the same franchise. She then produces these items for a refund, and even has a receipt for proof (if it's even asked for, if not, this scam is even more profitable than you might think). The crook gets her money back again, that makes it twice now for about an hour's work.

Here's the beauty. Even if she takes the receipt, the crook, if she does this just once a day, five day's a week "needing" the weekend off after a hard week's work would average about $400.00 a scam (that's about the amount I dealt with), that she takes home, tax free, $96,000.00 a year. Remember how much I told you I was making as a rookie? Hang on, it gets worse.

Let's say the crook gets caught at stores a little too close to each other. One manager calls another and she enters the store and the sharp employee calls the cops. We get there and, wait a minute, what's the crime? If they weren't caught shoplifting, all they're doing is returning the very same product they "paid" for, "here officer, I have a receipt." If we can't prove the item is stolen (and it probably won't be if they weren't caught) then we have no "arrestable, knowledgeable crime" and we have no choice but to say bye-bye.

Let's say we find a good reason to arrest them. Mine signed a false name on the refund slip, complete with a local address that doesn't exist, and lied to me to boot, that's obstructing! Cuff her

Dougo! I did, but the work just started. I have to find enough of a trail that I can prove, in a court of law, that what could "look" legal, is not. Bring in the $1,200 suits, you'll see mentioned often in these words, and my work has just begun. Let's cut to the chase. I've called in a zillion store managers, proven the bad guy did wrong, and they get sentenced to prison. You'll probably spend more time finishing this book than the bad guy will spend in jail. After all, it's non-violent, a property crime only and, remember what you've heard again and again, the prisons are so overcrowded that only the "really" violent can ever even expect mail at their local house of corrections. Enough said–you see the risk vs. the reward ideology.

In Lincoln, Nebraska, a sentence handed down by a District Court judge was overturned, (naturally) by the Court of Appeals, because the judge used a line of biblical scripture during the sentencing phase. It's not a wonder our kids can't pray in school if a judicial servant of the public can't follow up on the same premise that was utilized to ensure all involved spoke the truth. We can swear to be honest, so help us God, yet we can actually appeal the sentence if His name or words dare to be spoken again.

In the nearest metropolis that connects my jurisdiction, the wonderful City of Tulsa, Oklahoma, a well known judge, bordering on infamous, had a case re-tried because he stated the defendant was presumed "not guilty," as opposed to "innocent," during the opening admonitions to the jury. Naturally, the "save the bad guys" Court of Appeals agreed and, as you can guess, every defense attorney that ever approached his bar scoured the transcripts and a mountain of cases were re-tried. It may seem trivial, but, I saw the fortunes of tax dollars that were thrown away thanks to the appellate court saying, "Uh oh, naughty-naughty, bad judge." You (the criminal) get another chance to destroy the public's faith in the criminal justice system, the same one that is our only recourse to solving an injustice and putting the bad guy away.

If murder cases can be re-tried due to elementary wording, and it matters not in the eyes of the appellate judges that every soul in the courtroom obviously understood that "not guilty" and "innocent" mean exactly the same thing, then our desire to serve justice is driven by ignorance and bolstered by the arrogance of appellate justices.

Just as a true law enforcement professional controls his/her emotions with the public, I must control my emotions while writing about the law. Allow me to stress that I live for the law and to support the laws. I can quote law with the best, however, the interpretation of the law is where we all agree to disagree.

What justice is served by my quoting what is written in statutes yet fail to convey what the root meaning was meant to imply? Could I have said that more plainly? Yes. Why not use plain English? Herein lies the reason for the legal double talk, the mumble jumble if you will.

An example. We all know that a red octagonal sign, with white lettering, bearing the most simplistic of words, means to hit the brakes, stop going forward momentarily, then be back on your way. The stop sign means stop your car, look both ways and, if all is clear, then go. That's easy enough. Well come on in, Mr. Law.

We must now stop a certain distance from the stop sign, with due regard to circumstances, yet not too close to the intersection and without braking in a manner that would imply that we were speeding in the first place. If the law was written merely to say "stop," well, then that would be easy. "Your Honor, I did stop."

Granted, you could have stopped three miles prior to the actual sign, but you did stop. Uh-oh, now we must interpret when you stopped. It really doesn't matter when you stopped, or even if you stopped, unless a problem happens, or, if you're caught not doing it.

If you're in a car wreck, where you stopped, if you stopped, is a vital piece of evidence. If you went around the school bus that was bearing its own stop sign, complete with flashing lights and you hit a child crossing the street that octagonal sign would take on a whole new meaning.

Hopefully, the gut wrenching pain that would follow such an incident would put the law so far away from your thoughts that the preservation of life would be the only concern. It should be, but that's only the beginning.

Lay aside the pain that the family of that innocent child will deal with, a pain that, commonly, will never fade. If the child dies, the family will never be a family again and you will be faced with the possibility of going to prison.

God, how big that stop sign is beginning to grow.

19

Now, to protect yourself, you must hire an attorney. You must, while hopefully dealing with the pain, prepare to rationalize, at about $80.00 an hour for the barristers of justice that don't yet have a reputation, why it wasn't your fault. You must now prove that you did stop, appropriately, and that you couldn't help what happened. Enter the legal, mumble jumble. If we have, in writing, exactly where to stop, when to stop, how to stop, they can prove, beyond a reasonable doubt, that you were right or wrong.

If you said at the scene of the wreck, while looking at the bleeding body of a child that could easily be your own, that it was your fault, it probably won't be admissible. The "heat of passion," at that moment, over-whelmed your emotions with words.

One attorney is trying to explain why the actions taken by the defendant deserve justice while the other attorney is pleading that a client of his/her stature is in need of the jury's sympathy.

For the attorneys out there that command $300 -$400 an hour (or more, if you can believe that), they'll tell you that an appropriately timed tear means the difference between guilt and innocence.

If for one second you don't believe that the defense goes to exorbitant lengths to "coach" a client (that's the bad guy in an expensive suit, looking none the part he did when we took him in), to tug at the heart strings of the jury, you're sadly mistaken. The difference in the manner of dress and vivid detail of the client's past service to the community is limited only to the defendant's bank account and the severity of the charge.

Let me stress that this is not a lawyer bashing text. Just as a bad cop is the ultimate of disgust, a good lawyer commands our utmost respect. To not only have knowledge about the myriad of laws they (and we) must know, they (we) must be able to convey that knowledge, in a very easy to understand manner, so that the jury not only isn't talked down to but felt to be a knowledgeable and vital cog in the legal process.

Remember, a jury is composed of teachers, retirees, and construction workers—"normal" folks. A law enforcement officer, and his/her family, will never be seated on a jury, just as a lawyer, on his own time, will most likely never see the inside of a jury box.

The reason, simply enough, is that those professions already have the inside on the legal process. Both, most assuredly, would be biased in their decisions. Those affiliated with the law enforcement process will want the death penalty for every crime and the other might wish leniency for the most heinous of acts.

Part of that, to a degree, is understandable. Every cop has seen those, admittedly guilty based upon the evidence as well as their own confession, set free.

Remember the first case I told you I "lost" in a court of law? It mattered not that he was intoxicated. He was. It mattered not that he possessed narcotics. He did. It mattered only, to the defense, that the numbers written on a piece of paper did not mirror the respective words written. The judge, free of any civil recourse for his/her rulings, right or wrong, must determine if the charges, as filed, had occurred, precisely. My words on the report stated he drove left of the centerline. The statue numbers, which remember we used for years, stated he drove left, which he did, of a center median, which he did not.

That was that. Case closed, charges dismissed, record clean. The next time he would get stopped there would be no mention that a past drunk driver, that admittedly used drugs, was seated behind the wheel.

Hours and hours of work, mounds of paperwork, involving everyone from the officer that made the arrest, to the detective that filed the charges, to the prosecutor that researched and prepared the case, all done a great expense to the taxpayers, all for nothing.

I personally wish that the law was there to try cases where there is doubt that a person committed an offense, not for the obviously guilty to beat the system.

Let's look at the subject that I just made reference to. Let's say what should have happened, specifically, that he was found guilty, happened. Without doubt, part of his sentence would be to obtain alcohol and drug (substance abuse) counseling. He obtains the needed help and, best case scenario, never commits the violation again.

Well, this time, "the system" failed him (he left the courtroom with a smirk on his face), he tells his buddies what a joke the law is, and now he doesn't fear the system.

Worst case scenario, he continues to drink to excess, gets high on his drugs but, this time, after he climbs behind the wheel, an officer doesn't find him before he has a wreck. He injures/kills/maims/beheads/cripples (name it, they all happen, every day) himself, others, or both.

Maybe, just maybe, the defense that unjustly arranged for his release, both from custody as well as the needed treatment, feels a little remorse that this was allowed to happen again. I just imagine that if the defense was held liable for the results of their courtroom dramatics, justice might take on a whole a new meaning, or, those now faded ideals of justice would return to the days of studying for the bar.

Now, before those reading this book begin to picture me as a callous, "hang 'em all" kinda person, I'm not. I go above and beyond to treat those I've arrested with understanding and, to a degree given the circumstances, respectfully.

I know they don't want to be there, often they got their "beer muscles" on and, add that to adrenaline laced defense mechanisms and often those that committed the given offense will say and do things that they really don't mean.

A true judge of character is how they act the next morning. Though still understandably uncomfortable with the surroundings, if they were treated properly, they are beating themselves up inside to the point that whatever you say will never be forgotten. They cling to every word as a child would when being scolded for the first time.

It is for this reason that it is fundamentally vital, and I stress *vital*, that your words as an officer help to foster repentance and rebuilding and not preach about the obvious. You will not be given a better opportunity to help, and that's why we became cops in the first place.

Likewise, you could forever destroy that person's conception of the police with inappropriate behavior or belittling statements.

Public relations can go a long way towards improving the community's perception of a cop's job, but it must be delivered with sincerity. Just as I can tell when I'm being lied to on the street, the public can perceive when your words or actions are based too much on the authority that comes with the badge and with not the heart that's directly behind it, but, back to the law.

We, the street cops, are given only one opportunity to enact on a situation, act appropriately, and go on. The suspect has afforded to them, almost to the point of being ridiculous, the following and then some. The initial arrest sequence, preliminary hearings, jury and non-jury trials, plea bargains, local/district/supreme court appellate and civil processes and so forth. If during any one of theses legal processes a technicality is found, or even presumed, the guilty may go free. Again, often the client's only setback will be limited to their current financial condition.

Bear in mind, while any or all of these processes are happening, you, the arresting officer, must be present to support your actions. It matters not that part-time employers are tired of your necessary absences and that the family is again neglected. Also ironic is that almost all of the processes occur during the "normal" working hours.

You don't arrest many intoxicated drivers during the normal hours because you work nights, after all, that's where the excitement is. So, work all night, be in court all day and then return to work at night, but, you'd better be well rested and sharp with your immediate decisions. Perfection isn't the goal; it's the expected standard.

Working with us to secure prosecution of the bad guys is the District Attorney's Office. A practicing assistant district attorney doesn't fair much better than a cop when it comes to salary. Years of law school, and a very demanding school at that, leaves the new attorney seriously in debt. He/she won't make enough in the DA's office to repay that debt while trying to survive. Hence, the alluring aspect of making in a week, in the private sector, more than all your years of service to the community combined can be a realistic distraction.

The private attorney makes a percentage on civil settlements, which can add up to a fortune depending upon how badly their clients were ill-treated or injured. All for writing fancy words on paper and acting for the court.

Ironically, at least for established attorneys, a majority of the work will be researched by salaried new attorneys or paralegals, and prepared by office staff and the credit goes to the law firm or partner as well as a lion's share of the monetary reward.

No one on this planet will ever convince me that any amount of legal mumbo jumbo justifies some of the multi-million dollar fees that are awarded to private lawyers. Even those working "in the interest" of the indigent or incarcerated bring home ridiculous fees, all with the clients best interest suggestively being their driving force.

One local attorney continues to make headlines for his "work" in reforming correctional institutions. The attorney loves to berate the system, tell how cruel and unusual treatment is administered for often the most frivolous of reasons and yet, recently published, was the hundreds of thousands of dollars he has received from the state government in payment.

If you want to sue someone who committed vile acts against your client, then I'll support you with my last breath. You try to sue for your client's rights to smoke marijuana or to consume other controlled substances (drugs), all hidden behind the pretext of religious freedom; I've got a problem with that.

Let me give you but one example of the endless lawsuits that hit our courts, daily. The following was taken directly from written text but I'll change the names just to be safe. With six months left to serve on a seven-year prison sentence, John feared, due to his confinement in prison, that his driving skills had deteriorated, and that he would be a public menace on the road when released from the pen.

When prison officials said (correctly) "no way," to his request for driving lessons, John sued. You guessed it. Incredibly, he won!

The court ruled he should be allowed to drive a car twice a week, outside the prison compound, to assure his driving was up to par when he was released.

I wish I knew if he was in prison for taking a life while driving drunk. Wouldn't surprise me a bit.

It's important that we all have the inalienable right to protect ourselves through litigation, but, the driving force must be born from a wrong, not from the system's ability to allow any idea to be construed as a civil or criminal violation.

I will defend with my life the civil rights of every man, woman and child. I will likewise fight, with all my abilities, against a civil rights organization that creates an alleged civil rights violation where there is none. Or even worse, on "behalf" of one who doesn't agree with that organization's philosophy, but merely uses their situation to gain publicity, usually for an unrelated cause.

And now let's jump on the plea bargain issue that is afforded to damn near anybody charged with a crime. Short of minor (hopefully first-time) offenses, where leniency and the opportunity to right a wrong is justified, usually through community service or a deferment, pleading out of a situation has gotten out of hand.

Granted, without a plea bargain opportunity our already bulging court dockets would be swallowed up, but, to reduce or dismiss altogether serious crimes, just so a minor offense will be quickly pled out is unacceptable.

Time after time I see serious, violent crimes, such as aggravated battery, reduced to simple battery or even assault. Does this not plant the seed of leniency, possibly for future offenses, into the mind-set of the defendant? Often, and this is a sad fact, we (the police) will present as many charges as we possibly can, knowing full well that half will be dropped anyway, leaving at least a few for the bad guy to pick and choose what he/she is willing to plead out to.

This is not a slam against the prosecution or the criminal justice system itself, just a problem that is gaining momentum. The prosecution's hands are tied as well.

I arrested a subject that was driving under the influence and, while beginning to handcuff him the fight was on. If I recall correctly, this was the suspect's fourth alcohol related offense and his second time to physically resist a police officer. I threw him over my shoulder (got lucky, just saw a Jackie Chan movie), he hit the ground, tried to kick me where my children of the future hope to begin, bruised my thigh (that's not hard with my thighs!) and he was secured and I took him away.

District charges were preferred, the case was solid and the subject pled to the (felony) alcohol-related offense, with the battery on this officer dismissed (no serious injury). He received four years in prison, due in large part to being an alumnus of the Department of Corrections. I was satisfied with that. Until, I was advised that of his four year sentence, with none of those years suspended by the way, due to a lengthy criminal history, he actually served far less than that. Ok, that's expected, but guess how much actual time he spent "inside" the prison system? *Fourteen days!*

Four-year sentence, two weeks actually served. Now that's a deterrent, ain't it?

The main reason for this all too common scenario? Prison space, or more accurately, the lack thereof.

25

I used to joke that if ever elected governor, I'd be in office for about a week, if that. Why, you say? Because I'd bankrupt the state by building more prisons than Wal-Mart has stores.

Every prison in the nation seems too overcrowded, affording the non-violent a quick out. Well, once the non-violent are free we still have overcrowding, so, when then release the "not so violent," leaving space for the really violent.

Uh-oh, still overcrowded. Now we're forced to release the really violent to leave room for the murderers. If for one minute you don't think a drunk driver isn't violent, just because he/she didn't have an accident or kill somebody "this time," you're sadly mistaken.

Just heard something a little disturbing on the TV. Per the source, 57% of the shows on television, not counting news and sports, have serious violence related content.

Well, I'm not about to jump on the take violence off TV bandwagon. Let's be realistic. Heck, I enjoy them as much as the next guy. The disturbing part was that 73% of the bad guys "got away" with crime.

If the idea that your actions, regardless how severe, will result in no punishment, the groundwork has been instilled in our youth that there's no need to fear reprisal. And that's just TV. It's a shame how closely that mirrors real life.

Try this out for a spin. If a $1,200 suit saves a life from prison, he'll command a king's ransom. If a cop saves a life, and I mean the breath from your lungs filling those of a lifeless body, we'll still have a problem paying our mortgage.

Let me give you another example of those "public minded, help the unfortunate," lawyers. Not too long ago, a chemical plant had a sulfur leak that resulted in a gaseous cloud covering parts of an innocent city. I recently saw a re-cap of the events on TV, "60 minutes" I believe, but the topic was not on the injured, but the lawyers that fled to the city in droves.

Reportedly, representatives of the law firms/agencies were contacting anyone and everyone that could have been involved, directly or indirectly. Eventually, the lawsuit involves some 65,000 folks and the settlement resulted in a $160,000,000 agreement. Of the several thousand dollars each recipient received, guess what the take was for the disaster leeches.

Approximately *$50,000,000.00.*

Literally millions of dollars, all for filing a few papers, and they never even had a full-blown trial. Ironically, many of the "victims" that were hounded for their addresses refused to pursue the matter. Why? Because a few folks were honest enough to say they weren't injured, physically or otherwise.

The other side of the coin, and the one that feeds these $1,200 suits, were those that had absolutely no contact with the tragedy yet came from dens everywhere and asked what line to stand in to get their money, and thanks to the bottom dwellers, they got it. Truly sad.

I'm no historian, however, I grew up hearing the name Clarence Darrow. Turned out to be a lawyer. Though I admittedly don't have all the facts that led to his notoriety, I do know that he'd never survive as a lawyer today. Why? Because he reportedly never turned down a client or charged a fee if that client couldn't afford it.

Apparently his motivation, which is prehistoric in relation to almost all of today's lawyers, was to defend for a reason and to right a wrong.

Justice, what a novel idea when it comes to the field of Law.

CHAPTER THREE
The Drunk Driver

In June-July of 1985, I observed eight traffic related fatalities during a forty-five day period. All but one was the result of drinking and driving. I have built a career on the relentless pursuit of detecting and apprehending the intoxicated driver. With experience comes confidence and with confidence grows expertise. Teaching and enforcing drunk driving statutes is my specialty.

I truly believe that even the "Dream Team" would buckle under the pressure if forced to defend one of my DUI alumni. Overly cocky? You bet!

I recall a Tulsa Police Officer preparing to give testimony on an alcohol-related arrest. The officer, Bob Hidelage, was the cop's cop when it came to alcohol and drug related impairment. When the prosecuting attorney began the case, the initial foundation was based on Officer Hidelage's experience. It must have taken fifteen minutes just to relay to the court his extensive abilities, training, instruction and experience. Never had I been so impressed and jealous at the same time. I swore that one day I'd obtain that level of professionalism.

Bob still works the streets in Tulsa, Oklahoma, and I'm continuing to strive to reach his level. It may never happen, but that's okay, too. The point is my internal desire to grow is as strong as ever and professionals like Mr. Hidelage continue to inspire us all.

As my DUI arrests mounted, public notice followed. Once the public became aware, I then was approached by several wonderful organizations including Mothers Against Drunk Driving, Victim's Impact Panels and, in my City of Owasso, Oklahoma, the Early Intervention Service Program.

I knew immediately that public speaking was one way that I could help others, if given the chance and I took that chance at every opportunity, again with my family suffering.

When I speak I have the opportunity to maybe, just maybe, reach that one person that will think twice before operating a vehicle and placing so many in harm's way. On the other hand, while I am spending the evening in front of a bunch of strangers, my family is again placed as second priority and neglected. This is far too common a scenario for every law enforcement professional.

Succeed at work, suffer at home. Succeed at home and limit your career potential. If anyone finds a harmonious antidote to cure one without the other suffering a side effect, please let me know.

In February 1997, I was given the Don Byerly award for achievements in the area of DUI enforcement. The namesake of this award was a Tulsa police officer who lost his life in the line of duty, at the hands of an intoxicated driver.

Though I've been blessed with more awards than I deserve, nothing could replace the sense of accomplishment I felt when my peers said, "Good Job," for that which had been, and still is, such a huge part of my life.

It is sadly ironic, however, that I believe had it not been for those mangled bodies back in '85, subconsciously rendering an indelible impression in my mind during my "pup" years, that I might not have devoted my career to the detection, apprehension and prosecution of the intoxicated driver.

Let me throw a few facts to you. The average drunk driver commits the violation about *eighty times a year.*

Even worse, and this is supported by a nationwide survey, for every four drunk drivers that come into contact with an officer, *three* are released. That's a fact.

Why? No police officer wants to arrest an offender, only to see them not register intoxicated, at least by legal standards, and then have to tap dance around a false arrest claim. Look out! Here comes the carpet again if your decision was wrong and they complain. Yet another reason for you to maintain good relations with all persons contacted.

You arrest the violator for their benefit, as well as the general public. It's a hard pitch to deliver with even the best of communications skills, and impossible if not working in concert with sincerity.

Being certified nationally to instruct Standardized Field Sobriety Testing/DUI detection, I get a real charge out of teaching the newest of the nation's finest to gain confidence when encountering an intoxicated driver. If applied properly, no drunk will be able to talk his/her way out of *my* back seat. That's how good the standardized tests are, even in the eyes of the most limp-wristed appellate court. This is an interesting bit of trivia. I used to wonder why, in hindsight, so many older gentlemen that I would stop for drunk driving had either runny or itchy noses. They just wouldn't leave their noses alone. I eventually found out that, in the old days, drunk driver tests usually consisted of touching your finger to your nose. Well, in anticipation of this test, the subject, instead of wiping or scratching their nose, were actually pinching the hell out of it.

When the officer started the test, the drunk knows exactly where to go. If there was a doubt about his level of intoxication, and they bluffed you by passing your tests they were released and allowed to go on their merry way.

Also, along the same line, don't think for a minute that a striped line on the floor of your local neighborhood tavern is there just to add to the ambiance. It's a practice strip, hoping that, with practice, you can bluff your way out the next police contact.

Well folks, you can practice 24 hours a day and it won't help you with my tests. If you dare to drive intoxicated on my streets, I promise to provide the chaser.

I'll not go into the specifics of each of the three tests, merely to let you know that they are exist, they do work, and you can't win against them. You think of that the next time you see a cruiser behind you and you've had "two" beers.

Often, while speaking to a group of first time DUI/DWI offenders, I am joined by those that been touched with tragedy, in the past, due to the actions of an intoxicated driver.

These souls live to teach and share heartbreaking stories of shattered lives in order to prevent more such tragedies. People like Gary Henderson, who lost his precious daughter, and Ray Hollingshead, who lost his dear son. Each are now affiliated with Mothers Against Drunk Drivers. They work tirelessly to help, for no compensation, short of the sincere desire that someone listening to the pain they bear every day won't get behind that wheel.

This is a timely place to pass something on. I just got home from work (17 hours, not too bad) and, before I started my shift last night, I spoke to the local monthly group of first time DUI offenders as well as the juveniles that were caught doing something they shouldn't have and they were sentenced to attend.

I was pleased to see Ray there (he's all over the state) and he started things off, reliving every slide that he maintains as a living shrine to his son, and his never-ending cause. After Ray spoke, I followed and, at my prodding, I even talked one our city paramedics (and a reserve police officer) into speaking.

Upon the conclusion, all those that participated, and any allowed guests, are requested to fill out a critique of what they heard. Just to say in their own words what was beneficial and, likewise, what wasn't. We enjoy reading the comments and, for the most part, they're very supportive of our efforts. These remarks help us to do better job the next time we get the opportunity to speak.

Two such remarks on this evening kinda tell the whole story. One sheet was filled out by a juvenile that bluntly said, "All cops are liars, so I didn't listen." He ended by saying, "They should have had this on Monday so it wouldn't have ruined my whole week."

Sadly, I was there to help, I didn't lie and, truthfully, I may never be able to reach this kid. At least I did try.

The second person was the reason I do what I do, but, so was that juvenile that branded me a liar. He was an elderly gentleman and, though the face was familiar, I couldn't recall the arrest. He removed his hat, offered his hand to me and I gladly extended mine. He said, clear and plainly, "I hated you for arresting me last month. I hated you all month. Now, I can never thank you enough, and for what's it worth, I was wrong." That quick, that simple and he vanished. I wish I could have told that man what those words were worth to me, to Ray and Gary, to everybody else that cares enough to do something about trying to fix it.

There are thousands that, like Gary and Ray, had to pay the ultimate price to bring you their individual story of pain. All the incidents are true, the pain is real and, though each story is sadly unique, all maintain a common theme.

Drinking and driving is a 100% preventable crime. You are neither forced nor compelled to drive drunk. Yet, ironically, you not only request but also possibly expect to find a sympathetic ear if you put yourself in that position. When you say, "I would give anything to take it back," or, "I would never intentionally hurt anybody, I'm a loving parent, etc.," your words are true, but, you made the choice and you have only yourself to blame.

Sorry, I don't really need to hear what bad luck you're having. Believe me, I've heard them all, and usually, when I find you driving drunk, you wind up blaming me. The bills are overdue, you're getting a divorce, you lost your job–you name it, I've heard it.

I really do care, but, no, I'm not letting you go. Get mad at me if you want, but I promise, when you wake up tomorrow, you'll at least be alive to get mad, and so will everyone else that would have driven your part of the road. I can live with that outcome.

Some folks need help staying on the straight and narrow. I want to share the ultimate fix for those agencies truly wanting a simple and very effective deterrent to crime. In fact, I've never seen nor heard of anything so simple, and legal, that it really makes local folks afraid to break the law in their hometown.

It's called the local newspaper.

In fact, here, the smaller the town, and fittingly the smaller the newspaper, the better. Why, you say? Well, I guess the smaller newspapers are hungry for articles to print and, as a result, they turn to the local police beat.

When I moved to Owasso, the paper printed every single arrest (adult only, that is, at the time), name for name and charge for charge, all in unsympathetic black and white. Though the local paper eventually stopped printing the police beat in favor of more national news, yet years later local residents still routinely ask, "Is this going to be in the paper?" Well, the paper started adding a section dedicated to the police again, and, true to form, the fear has returned at the thought of your upstanding name appearing with the morning paper and cup of coffee at Fred & Wilma's next door.

Nothing brought more fear to their souls than the prospect of their lapse from the straight and narrow being read by every neighbor, every co-worker, their priest, employer, you name it. It is a truly effective way to scare the "crime" out of future would-be backsliders.

No, my desire is not kick you when you're down. But, hopefully you don't allow yourself to fall to begin with if a seed of deterrence has already been planted. It helps keep the good guys good and it put pressure on those with real problems to keep on the wagon or get help.

One of the first tasks I encountered, while a reserve deputy sheriff, was to respond to a signal 82, possible signal 30. That means an injury accident with possible fatalities. Upon our arrival we found the cars, we found the evidence of alcoholic beverages involved and, I'll never forget this, we found the lifeless body of an infant. Bad enough? Yes, but that wasn't the worst.

Missing from that innocent victim of this sickness was a leg. A tiny human being, innocent-from-wrong, less a body part. Did you figure out what my job was?

That's right. I was told to find that leg, which I did, and the most charismatic of authors could never do justice to the raw sense of waste I felt when I found it, about the weight of a small bass. A truly sick comparison, but I had a job to do, and I did it. God knows I'll live with the thought of that night for the rest of my life, but, if I do my job right, you'll never know it.

I'm not allowed to remember it and you'll surely complain on me if I do. Heck of a way to start a career, and I'm volunteering my time to do this. It's then that you question the path you have chosen, and hopefully, you finally then understand that you have what it takes.

That doesn't stop you from screaming into a pillow when you get home, nor will it prevent the nightmares that are sure to come. The job does, however, have to be done and no force in the world can stop you from your chosen life's work.

Please, whatever you do, don't think about that obvious drunk you've all seen on the road and say, "I could find drunk drivers. I oughta be a cop." If those no-brainers were all it entailed then you're right, you could. A small and I mean very, small percentage of intoxicated drivers are gimmees. More often than not, only one or two very minor "clues" will be observed.

Any defense attorney, even those greener than grass to a courtroom, can easily justify why that small infraction(s) occurred. Bad roads is a common ploy, but generally, they hit you with the "Oh, so you never make a mistake driving, officer?" Catch twenty-two here. If you say no you're either a liar or not human, neither of which are too appealing from the eyes of a jury box. Kinda like the old adage, "Have you stopped beating your wife?" No way to answer that with a yes or no, either way, you're a wife beater.

Got one for you. A personal bit of philosophy, if you will. Murder is defined as the premeditated taking of a human life by another. If you drink, you realize that the alcohol will effect you. In many instances, impairment or intoxication is the desired result, or in other words, your premeditated goal.

Now get behind the wheel, turn the ignition, drive while impaired and have a wreck, taking a human life. Your premeditated actions resulted in the taking of a human life. Food for thought?

How many of you out there (no need to raise your hands), have driven a car, either drunk or while drinking, in the last year?

I'll tell you this. You want to see how much life can change, the real meaning of fear, then put yourself in that position. The thought of being told to put your hands behind your back and feeling the imprisonment of handcuffs is a nightmare that you'll never wake up from.

The drive to the police department, the questions you must answer, seeing your personal property thrown on a table in front of you, pretty harsh stuff. And that doesn't touch the "long walk" to your new home, a cell, and looking at the hardened faces and deadly stares of your new roommates. You'll never forget this night, I hope. For most, once is all it will take. That's why I try to respect your fears and offer any help to ensure this nightmare is not repeated.

It used to be a joke that I could arrest a guy (or gal), tow his car, write him a zillion tickets, take away his license, put him in jail and, when he got out, he'd offer to buy my dinner. A fellow employee, Bill "No Neck" Mozingo, said that he couldn't give a warning without pissing someone off. Einstein would have blown a blood vessel if he had tried to figure out Mo. That's Mo, God bless him. I'll talk more about him later.

The point is, despite the severity of the actions (and few are more severe than drunk driving) you must treat the suspect as a person. All but the most habitual offenders, and I'll talk about those bastards later, need help. I don't mean counseling for every offender nor are Hail Mary's a requirement. A desire to ensure that mistake, that hopefully didn't necessitate an officer hunting for the body part or organ of one of our precious children, is but an unspeakable story that will never again be told.

I'll do what I can for the first timer, and then some, but dare grace my presence again with the odor of death on your breath, and you'll wish the devil himself was your defense attorney. And, by the way, I'd kick his ass in a courtroom too.

When will I ease my relentless pursuit of the intoxicated driver? I'll tell you. When, and only when, I've wiped away the last of the blood from the hands and healed the wounds from the souls of every law enforcement officer that has had to clean up the pain drunk drivers have so carelessly caused, then, and not before, will I be allowed to find ways to better serve the community I so dearly love.

That was heavy, I know. I'll not apologize because I meant every word, but I want you to not only feel the ugly side of wearing a badge but the wonderful breath of life it offers as well. You'll find it later in this book, but, not in this chapter.

I was told of a lawsuit that is, or was, pending in an appellate court. It dealt with a very well-to-do gentleman that, while highly intoxicated, drove his Lexus into the side of an older model station wagon. True to the sick pattern that governs DUI reality, the drunk escaped with minor injuries.

The occupants of the station wagon, a mother and her two only children, were dead at the scene.

A lawsuit was filed. Well, now that's why we have lawyers, right? Wrong. The lawsuit was filed on behalf of the gentleman that killed the innocent mother and her even more so innocent children.

The basis of the lawsuit, sick as it may be, was that the inspection sticker on the station wagon was expired. Thus, in the eyes of the defense, "they" stated the accident "might" have been prevented if the vehicle was properly inspected, hinting that the expired inspection sticker indicated that the vehicle was unsafe, thereby potentially leading to the accident.

It gets worse...

Now get this. A man loses his wife and his only children, in other words his family, at the hands of a drunk driver, and he has to defend himself in court.

Just so we all understand...You must now pay for the services of a lawyer, that you can ill well afford, owning only an older model vehicle that was destroyed along with your family whom you just buried. You already owe the undertaker for the triple funeral and now your family's murderer is suing you because your inspection sticker was expired.

You tell me something that makes any form of common sense and decency in this most twisted of scenarios, and convince me it's the right thing to do, and I'll give you my badge.

I told you we'd talk about the true bastards of driving drunk, the habitual offender. You'll find few more callous. They have one of two personalities. They are either the nicest people you've ever met or it's a fight (usually just mouthy) from the traffic stop to the jail cell.

They've been through it before, know the routine and it's no longer a fear, just an inconvenience. They know all about bail bondsman, what you (the cop) can and can't do and exactly what it takes to get back on the street. They refuse the state's test(s), which means their license is automatically suspended (save, of course, for the ever protecting the bad guy, appellate courts), but they couldn't care less. They haven't had a valid driver's license since God knows when anyway.

Their thoughts are nowhere near that long since void piece of laminate that bears a much younger photo likeness of better times.

As I stated earlier, the average drunk driver, drives drunk, an average of eighty times a year. The habitual offender, double that, maybe triple. Depends how many days there are in a year and how many times his or her refrigerator lies empty.

If they haven't taken a life then they're trying awfully hard to do so, whether they know it or not. They have the same sense of immortality as the sociopathic teenager. Add experience of "the system" and they've got absolutely no fear. Many don't even fear a police cruiser that just started following them.

They usually have a problem driving sober, on those rare occasions, so they're actually in their natural habitat. Even if they do get stopped they are back to scratching their nose and teaching that young cop a thing or two about how to do their job.

Usually, they shower the protector of the weak and innocent with glowing compliments of how he could never fill a cop's shoes. That works a lot of times, believe it or not.

Too often, "drive home safely and be careful" are the last words he hears, while he gets back into his deadly weapon and gains yet even more confidence in beating the boys and girls in blue.

Being a habitual drunk driver, you have contempt not only for the system, but also for life as well. Your only desires are personal, and diseased, living to and for your pleasure.

You sound real convincing to a Pardon and Parole Board when you talk of the growth, and usually religion, that you've found while on your short prison stay. Actually, you're probably being sincere. Your force-fed "drying out period" cleared your brain cells enough to motivate your intent on living the way "the good Lord told you to," or so you say to the Board.

An overcrowded prison system with a good floorshow and bingo! You're back on the streets armed to kill again.

Just like the District Attorney's office, and, to a VERY, VERY slight degree the Appellate Court Justices, the Pardon and Parole Board Members have their hands tied.

We can't keep the deserving locked up because we have no room in our prisons. We can't build the prisons to hold them because the costs are too high and the taxpayers, or respective state budget(s), can't either rationalize, justify or finance building more.

To a degree, I understand. Your streets are full of potholes, you need another school or the local and state supported agencies are going to close due to a lack of funds.

You have to put the money somewhere and, though we all agree we need the prisons, it's highly unlikely the occupants of those cells will ever walk the streets that *we* live on.

I guess that false sense of security lingers in the back of all our minds when the privacy of a ballot box shrouds our fears. The immediate neighborhood needs are vital and the big picture is suddenly clouded when the sanctity of the voting booth curtains are closed.

That's but one of the obviously sad reasons that the habitual, potential killers are still living next door. They'll continue to do so until the severity of their "premeditated" crimes are taken at face value.

Sadly, in the eyes of the court, if you kill with a gun you're a murderer. If you kill with a car, while driving drunk, you had an accident. Though I pray that an appellate court judge doesn't feel the pain of losing a child at the hands of a drunk driver, I bet you could clock with an egg timer, if one of their family falls at the hands of an intoxicated driver, how long it takes for this crime to be given its due level of severity in the eyes of the law.

Though I've always wanted to write a book, to give an insight into my opinion of being a cop on today's streets, I really hope this book sells enough copies that I could afford to really pursue a socially worthwhile goal. I would love to spend a couple of months, or even a couple or years, to live inside the baron souls of the habitual drunk driver.

I'd live in the prisons. I'd eat the TV dinners in their modest homes and apartments, anything to actually learn what it would be like to live as one that I so despise. Maybe that insight would afford the social agencies the true ammunition they need to defeat this plight and, just maybe, arm the criminal justice system with the ability to re-write the laws so that a true habitual offender becomes as extinct today as the dinosaurs are in our history books.

You can never truly stop someone from driving a vehicle while drunk unless they have nothing to consume to get in that condition.

Since it's highly unlikely a global-wide prohibition is on its way, (Nor would I want it. I enjoy a beer or two in the privacy of my own home as much as the next man.) I suggest we all take a more active stance, from the home front, to let them know how close tragedy really is.

Granted, it would take a gazillion dollars to blanket the TV screens with proof it could happen, to the point the potential offenders/victims actually believe it, before many might give it a second thought. But, what a nice dream. For it to become commonplace to think, "I wonder who could drive me home," Wouldn't that be a lifesaver?–to have the idea that driving drunk is as criminal and wrong as murder. That, in my opinion, is what it's going to take.

Until then, I'll keep doing my job, catching them hopefully before they unwittingly strike, or, and I hate this part, covering up the lifeless bodies when we don't.

Please allow me lay on another all too common episode in our daily duties, though admittedly, this is pretty extreme. It's a decade plus old and another one of those that makes you wonder why we do what we do. I'll never forget it.

We were requested, by the Department of Public Safety, to deliver a death message to a lady who just became a widow, though she had no idea.

Her husband, as I learned later to be a very good and caring man, drove drunk, rolled his pickup off a hill and was crushed to death.

I watched as the seasoned officer told this wonderful person that her husband of thirty-four years would not be coming home.

You can't say, "I know how you feel," because you don't. If you haven't been in that position don't act like you have, even if you're sincere and desire only to bring comfort.

I'll say this. She was a strong lady, even felt sorry for us that we had the job of telling her. Quite a lady.

Well, we waited for a couple of hours for family members to arrive, to be with her at the time when her soul is gasping for support and we heard the first car arrive. I go to meet her family and I'm greeted with the sight of a state trooper, in the company of a chaplain.

Thank God, the pro's are here! After the introductions I tell them she's doing well, exceptionally well given the circumstances and that we're waiting on family members. A puzzled look later confirms that they had no idea what I was there for, much less what I was talking about.

It turns out this newest of widows had but one son and, at the far end of the same state her husband just left, her son had been killed by a drunk driver. The same day, within ninety minutes of each other, her entire reason for living had been stolen at the hands of drunk drivers.

I've never seen or even imagined that so much pain could fall on one person, especially one that had done no wrong and deserved only the finest things life had to offer. Since words will only disgrace the gravity of what occurred, I'll not say another word about it, at least here.

I'll continue to preach this story every time I greet first time offenders, for if her pain won't make one think, they're beyond hope at my level.

To add one point, this is but one reason we, in the law enforcement families, hold but the utmost respect for state troopers (state police).

Every cop will occasionally deliver a death message, but, to our state's first line of defense, this all too typical scenario is but a daily ritual.

How would you envy having breakfast, starting your car and heading to the residence of neighbor just to look them in the eyes and tell them that a family member is dead.

What will help, you ask? Make the laws and penalties of driving intoxicated tough. Very tough.

I recently saw how the State of Georgia had greatly stiffened its drunk driving laws in the mid- 1990's. Did it help? Apparently. In 1995 and 1996, which are the latest figures available, they saw a decline in DUI arrests of 39%. That's a huge drop, for such a major problem, in a very short period of time.

The State of Louisiana has a great approach as well, though I don't have the legal mumbo-jumbo with me. It does, however, unlike our state, allow a law enforcement officer to stop a suspected intoxicated driver based solely on witness information.

They (Louisiana) feel that the minimal intrusion is far outweighed by the benefit to society. My state, like many others, have too many $1,200 suits that have probably never lost a loved one at the hands of some intoxicated driver who screams of their rights being violated.

We must first observe a violation regardless if you, the caring citizen, flagged us over to tell us of the cars that he/she ran off the road or how close they came to that bridge embankment.

I will tell of one "potentially promised" amendment that, without bragging (if you can believe that) I thought of years ago. A second conviction for driving drunk results in a possible vehicle forfeiture of their cherished automobile. That, if nothing else, for the many violators who could care less of a life not their own, might just think twice before starting what might as a result become ours.

The most obvious reason that drunk drivers always have, and always will exist, is simple. Alcohol, like any other substance that affects your central nervous system, impairs your thoughts, your actions, your mind-set. If your fears are minimized, your reactions are slowed and your judgement is clouded, would it not make sense that your physical motor skills are limited? Of course.

With your physio-motor skills limited, the depressant chemically reacts on the brain. It produces (if allowed) "beer muscles" in the otherwise timid and invincibility in the occasionally brazen.

Place those chemical factors in the bodies of those that are always jerks, sober or otherwise and the fight is on, if not at the bar, than on our traffic stop when we find them on our streets.

Though drinking and driving is no laughing matter, a few times in a career an incident comes along that just makes you shake your head, even laugh, if you can block the past pain.

In the days prior to my joining the Owasso force, I was told a story of a drunk driver that had driven off the road and come to a stop in a muddy ditch. When officers arrive at the scene, they find the driver slumped over the wheel, *passed out*, in other words.

The first officer at the scene finds the doors locked, the engine running at it's still in drive. When he finally succeeds in waking up the driver he, the bad guy, sees a uniform, gets a "double Spanky, Oh-No" look and slams the gear even lower and hits the gas pedal. Well, the tires do nothing but spin, fling mud and the drunk is actually trying to steer, apparently thinking he is making good with his get-a-way.

The officer, obviously a quick thinker and with my respect, began running in place and screaming for the suspect to "slow down," with the cop running in place faster, as the mud's flying farther.

With the drunk in total disbelief that a cop is keeping up with him he slams both feet on the brakes, the officer slows his pace of running in place and slowly stops bouncing, breathing heavily to intensify his dramatic performance. The drunk puts it in gear, unlocks the door and couldn't be more cooperative, for after all, he chased him down on foot. Don't want to make this cop mad!

Knowing habitual drunk drivers the way I do nowadays, I can promise you he (the suspect) has told that story even more times than we have (probably in a local drunk tank).

Another one I had a dealing with was a gentleman who hated life, hated us, and especially I think, himself. He was burdened at birth with a leg six inches shorter than the other and walked with a very prominent cane. He didn't look good on the outside because he hated how he looked on the inside. Anyway, he's driving drunk, I find him and before I can ask him to take my tests he's quick to point out he can't do them thanks to his "bum leg" and to (I'll never forget this) "take me in if you're man enough."

Well, I was, but, given his contempt for everything living, I was far from done. I told him to walk a line, he started in (very profanely) on his short leg, and I told him to put his good leg on the street and his short one on the curb and go, now.

He gives me a "what the hell have I gotten into" look, is apparently startled that his attitude and "handicap" didn't send us scurrying away and he heads to the curb. In fact, after a feeble attempt, and not due to his leg but to his state of intoxication, he gives a muffled giggle (probably the first time he even thought of a laugh in years) and simply walks to my patrol car, leans his cane against the door and puts his hands behind his back.

He'd been beaten at his own game, on his own grounds and, if never before or since, at least for one second he showed respect for the uniform, and not from out of fear.

Could I walk into a courtroom, let alone the police chief's carpet and say what I did was right? Probably not. It worked better than anything ever could have, at the time, but no, it wasn't really "right." I haven't done it since, nor will I, but, that's part of growing up. I have one more very, very personal insight that I hope will open your eyes as much as it did mine, and continues to this day.

This is important. In today's times I would be guilty of a crime and subject to arrest if what I'm about to tell you wasn't reported, to my supervisor's, immediately. At the time, nothing, but nothing could have served justice better. In fact, I tell this story to every recruit that I train, but, I still have to decide if it was right or wrong, and I leave that decision to the recruit as well (but I tell them to take a lot of time in coming to a decision).

Shortly after being sworn-in as a campus cop, I caught a drunk driver (naturally) and, since the campus didn't have a jail or holding facility, we took them to the city or county jail, dependent on the crime. Anyway, I arrive at the city booking area, place my drunk on the counter and a veteran officer, in every sense of the word, brought in a drunk that would make the most foul-mouthed sailor blush.

I was impressed that this veteran, gray haired cop could take so much verbal abuse (after all, the guy's handcuffed) and still look totally unaffected by it all. Well, this continued for at least ten minutes and, before being placed in a cell, the drunk had one final search. It got close enough to the "codules" that the drunk said to the cop, "Thank God you're a faggot, at least you'll suck my **** before I..."

Then it happened. All we heard, after "before I," was a loud clap, and Mr. Drunk was not only silent, and stunned, but apologetic. He had slight redness, resembling finger marks, on one cheek and only the dispatcher actually saw what happened. When the vet cop (I'd love to credit him with his name, but well, you understand) had his fill, at just a time when only a true veteran would know, he gave him one, open-handed, smack. Nowadays, that's illegal, and to a degree, rightfully so.

No mediator on this planet could have defused a potentially explosive situation so quickly, so appropriately. His open-handed hit was not meant to hurt, in fact, the opposite could be said. He saw a means of not only keeping the younger cop's in line, but he kept the drunk from going too far. By the way, all the other folks arrested that night were tuned in to every word.

Did he tell the younger cop's it's okay to hit a handcuffed prisoner? No. Did he tell a "veteran drunk" that he had gone too far and to sober up? Yes.

By the way, for those that don't know cops, the vet could have dismembered this guy before his first nerve signaled a problem was coming. I still can't give you a personal answer on right or wrong.

What the veteran officer did was to see a problem, select an option, act, and the situation is handled.

Today, if an officer sees another officer use excessive force, and yes, by statutes, if your bad guy is handcuffed and not Jackie Chan, that force includes everything from a slap down (even if you're trying to calm him/her down), every officer that witnesses, or hears, of that slap is mandated to report that action to a supervisor, immediately.

I never have, nor ever will, advocate the use of force when not called for. I also advocate, with all that is mine, using every force I can to protect my family, my uniformed family, the public I serve, and, yes, the bad guy that, in my custody, has just harmed one that I've sworn to serve, protect or back on a call.

CHAPTER FOUR
Juvenile Crime

The hot media news of today tells of how many innocent kids are being killed, not on those terrible streets, which they are, but in the *safety* of our public schools. In the good old days, we'd either personally drive our kids to school or we'd escort them to the security of that big, safe, yellow school bus. When we would see them safely on their way and a cloud of smoke meant our parental duties had been fulfilled for the morning. God, how far down has our society fallen?

Public schools in the United States expelled more than 6,000 students, in the last year alone, after they were caught with firearms on school grounds. We hear of a half a dozen atrocities involving students killing students and, for some reason, we seem to wonder in disbelief. What if all 6,000 had killed a fellow student, on the same day, then what would we do? Actually, that very scenario could have happened.

Usually, when you hear of a juvenile crime, you probably used to think of vandalism, curfew, throwing eggs, toilet papering a house or spray painting walls. Nowadays, especially lately, we're comforted if we find out a fourteen-year-old didn't take out his teacher and half of his classmates. Folks, this is a problem of paramount importance and, I promise you, we'd better take charge, and I mean now.

I will now paraphrase but one selection from the uniform crime reports distributed annually via the U.S. Department of Justice, and this deals with spray painting.

A 27-year veteran corporal with the Bayfield County Sheriff's Office (Wisconsin) was killed (in 1996) while investigating a report of vandalism. The officer was dispatched to investigate a report of the spray painting (kid's) of an apartment door. I would say you don't get much more juvenile, nor petty, than a call like that.

When the officer arrived at the scene (remember, a cop for 27 years) he entered the apartment building and began climbing the stairs in order to meet with the complainant. As he approached the top of the stairs, one of the apartment doors opened and a male exited. He allegedly began firing numerous shots at the officer from a .223-caliber automatic rifle. The man pointed his weapon at the complainant who was able to retreat unharmed into her apartment. The man resumed firing at the officer who had fallen to the bottom of the staircase; a total of thirty (30) rounds were fired. The officer, aged 57, was mortally wounded with injuries to the neck, head and chest. Shortly thereafter, the assailant committed suicide using the same weapon with which he had assaulted the victim officer.

I could speak for weeks, strike that, years, on what I feel about the juvenile criminal justice system. Again, just as I don't blame the governors for not building more prisons, I cannot, knowing what I do, blame the juvenile authorities for not keeping the "bad kids" locked up. I've arrested the same kid, week after week, for crimes that an adult would have done a "week's hard time" for.

The criminal statutes have the years printed that they, the offender, could (should) serve for a given crime. Nowadays, we should have two criminal statutes to use for reference material. One, as is currently written, would tell what the original legislator's demanded and what is "written on the books." The second, and this is the practical one, will tell what you'll actually know what one can expect to receive.

It's not a classified secret that every kid, at least those that know the law, expect nothing to occur until that magical transformation from childhood to manhood occurs, or in legal terms, emancipation. For the layman reading this, that means eighteen years old. Recent changes in the law have made serious crimes, depending on your given state, reverse certifiable. This means, and I love this, that a "child" will be held accountable for his/her crimes as an adult. Sadly, knowing as we all due that every possible appellate opportunity is crying for their attention, now they can appeal for their crime to be heard by a juvenile court. In other words, no penalty that is backed with the potential opportunity for real incarceration.

Do I want to put everybody in jail? No. Do I want those that know better, that commit crimes, especially those that hurt people and make our kids afraid to go to sleep at night or walk the school grounds, do I want them to sleep in a little cell? Yes. To afford protection to "children" that make mistakes is a very important part of legal process. To afford an always-available interstate to freedom for those that know better, I really hate that abuse of social caring.

In my days of youth, we would never, ever even think about showing disrespect to a law enforcement officer, let alone our parents. Today, more than you might think, we routinely see juveniles speak to mothers and fathers as if they were slaves, merely an adult body whose sole life function is to jump at their every command. Compound that with a parent that defends their child's actions, in front of the arresting officer, and you've just armed this "oh so innocent" offender with the ammunition to openly defy the system. The more times he/she has an experience with the law, and the parents respond as I've mentioned, the cockier their attitude, and respectively, the more daring or severe are their actions.

Though I won't make a lot of friends with this statement I feel, as do many of my brothers and sisters in uniform, that a majority of the blame must be laid directly at the feet of the parents. I don't mean just those parents that chide in with their kids that all we do is harass them. Apathy breeds contempt, both for the parents at home as well as the cops on the street. To give a child "their freedom," with no restraint on the reins, sub-consciously tells them, "You're an adult, so do as you wish." And to compound that problem, when they do get into trouble, you (the parent) utilize this opportunity to show your child how you will support then unconditionally. The lack of time you spent with them in the past is now negatively reinforced by, in a twisted sense of caring, coming to their defense. See where I'm going with this?

The only time you spend with them is when they've done wrong and then your only input is to get them released, to get them out of trouble. Your parental intentions may be valid, but your negative reinforcement is forever embedded in their minds, and merely manifests itself with each passing occurrence.

Please, whatever you (the parent) feel, don't think for one minute that your kids aren't playing with your parental loyalty and responsibilities. Certainly not all to the same degree, but, I'll tell you this from experience, many times I have arrested juveniles, often with "wanna-be" affiliations to gangs, and, given the rapport you've established, some will be "straight" with you. The cocky ones, those that have been through this several times, will tell you that all they need to do is "yes ma'am," look sympathetic and, given the severity of their situations, start to well up with the onset of tears. It works almost every time and some of these kids will brag how easy it is to manipulate their folks. It really gets bad when the parents fall for it, the kids know it and, I promise you, they are laughing on the inside as they head out the door.

Can I, the police, tell the folks what some of their kids are doing, even if they've told me themselves that they are just using their folks? In a word, no. Why? I'll tell you. We, the police, have known these kids for just a short time, in the worst of situations to begin a distant relationship and you, the parent, have raised them from birth. Who do you think, under these circumstances, will feel they know the intent of their respective kids' actions, leading up to our involvement, the best. Now, and this always happens, the offender lays the blame for his/her situation on their friends (associates) that were either arrested with them or got away. So now they have the support of the parents, the given charge is blamed on an associate, which reduced your child's involvement and we, the authorities, look like we have a personal vendetta against your kid for trying to pursue a serious violation of the law.

Let me tell you about a recent incident. I arrested several kids for grand larceny, with marijuana found on two of the three. As the respective parents arrived, they each listened intently to the voices in the lobby, trying to distinguish if Mom and Dad, hopefully Mom, have arrived.

One joked to the other, "Time for the floorshow." I inquired to one, who was fairly at ease speaking with me, exactly what he was planning for his floorshow. He speaks, quite confidently, that he'll show her the little boy she raised to go to Sunday school (they all laugh and agree, hitting knuckles in a sign of camaraderie), and blame the cops for their treatment and false allegations. One, and I'd love to say his name but can't do so, said, "No offense, Officer Doug, but if I don't blame you for being the jerk (certainly not limited to those words) then it's my ass that loses face." That blunt, that honest. I'll give him this much credit, at least for one brief moment, he was honest.

If I approach the folks with his admission, it really goes downhill. First, they'll deny it. That's real bad. To begin with, it takes away from the original reason that we caught them. Secondly, it makes our

47

actions look personal, which not only takes away from their actions but also questions the credibility of our actions. Thirdly, the offender will never take us into his confidence again, so we lose face on the street, often resulting in not getting information that we otherwise would have. Some might say, "Well then, just tape record the conversation and play it for the folks."

Well, that would help this one incident but, word would spread like wildfire and every booking process from that night, with any kid that thrives for that lifestyle, we'd be lucky to get a name, at least a real one. We might win that small battle but we'd lose every battle thereafter and eventually the war. Sorry, that was a little melodramatic for me to, but, the words are valid and the outcome would be disastrous.

Also, the song and dance routine the kids play with their folks goes for the boys in uniform, as well. I know I've been duped more than once and it really pisses me off. Trust me. As a rule, if the juvenile offender starts with either, "Can I talk to you in private?" or, "I swear to God," you can pretty much count on the rest of their words to be total garbage. The words and delivery are sincere, often worthy of an Oscar, but the content is limited to what they think we want to hear. You have a cop that falls for it, and often goes to superiors with the mistaken belief that he cleverly obtained this confidential and vital inside information, and the offender really gets a woody off of that. You, the officer, get embarrassed, your superiors lose faith in your judgments and the offender not only beat the cop but also learned a little bit more how to beat the system, while gaining even more confidence.

Please bear one very important fact in mind. To a large degree, the juvenile offenders of today are the adult criminals of tomorrow. The actions that we, the police and parents together take, will directly effect what the future holds in store for our children. No question that we all hope for them the most successful of lives, with *Little House on the Prairie* families and personal comforts that maybe we, the parents, never got to enjoy.

Sadly ironic, the actions, or usually the lack of, may be the contributing factor that inadvertently sends the future leaders of the country into the wrong direction. Don't get me wrong. We, the parents, hopefully did a good enough job in teaching right from wrong, at least for the basics. It's when the wrong is downplayed, the necessary discipline is either not administered or wrongly done so, that we must take at least partial blame for the actions of our kids. And don't forget, the failure to properly discipline (and I don't mean to beat here, but to discipline, which varies from standing in the corner to using a belt, you know which is appropriate), does, in part, lead to how each child will contemplate what path to choose.

There's one other group of "kids" that I'd like to address before moving on. How about those kids that seem to have everything against them, from the start. Poor neighborhoods, crime infestation, drug dealers living next door and, I really hate this one, parents that either down the police or even teach their kids to be afraid of us, from as early as they learn how to speak. We may never, ever be able to reach or help this group. I've stated earlier, I'm no psychologist. In a way, I'm glad. If I look at every action from a scientific point of view, I'll miss the human aspect, the gut feeling, and the reason for the spontaneity of their actions. These kids may be the recipients of a carton of cigarettes for their 16th birthday. If they go to school or not, the choice is theirs. It does happen and it's more common than you might think.

Let me tell you of one another scenario, dealing with juveniles, that occurred when I first joined the Owasso Police Department. I had arrested a 16-year-old boy on drug related charges. His father was no stranger to the law, having been arrested several times, all for either drug or alcohol related reasons. Prior to my joining the Owasso force, the father of this subject had successfully sued the City of Owasso for the improper serving of a narcotic search warrant. Yep, he had drugs, but the service of the warrant was improper in the eyes of the court (naturally, the appellate courts) and the city, as is common, settled out of court. The charges are dropped and the "bad guy" makes money for breaking the law. It's a common, quick fix within many, many cities and towns. Pay a smaller sum now, the matter goes away and usually the cop loses his job. If I recall correctly, he used the money for a new truck and enjoyed little more, I'm sure, than driving it past the police department, laughing all the way.

To continue, I summoned his father to the police department to assume custody of his son. Upon his arrival he was very polite, attempted to utter disbelief that his dear son would possess any "of that stuff" and he signed a release agreement, remanding his son into his custody. On the way out, just past the lobby, I heard him say, to the effect, "I can't believe you were stupid enough to hold grass where they could find it." The problem was not that he possessed, but that he got caught. Folks, I heard it myself.

Do we blame the juvenile for possessing drugs when all his dad cares about is that he got caught? From a legal standpoint, sure we do. From a realistic point of view, he merely erred in the ways that Dad had brought him up. If anything, his only remorse is in failing in the ways his father raised him, not in breaking the law by possessing, and using, drugs. Put aside another chapter on what drugs do the human body, but look at the negative reinforcement supplied by his father. Remember him, he's the one that teaches us right from wrong. Blame the child if you wish. I think good old Pop's the one that needs to be hammered on this one.

Before I had a chance to finish this book, "reverse certifiable" crimes had already changed. Now we have the Youthful Offender Act (YOA). Actually, this may be a step in the right direction. If a 15, 16, or 17-year-old commits one of twelve crimes, they are considered a youthful offender and treated the very same as an adult. These twelve crimes, primarily "the biggies," namely murder, robbery, sex crimes, arson and weapons violations (where injury/death is the premise) are included. The big change, and this is important, is that 16 and 17-year-old offenders will have to answer, as an adult, for burglary (first degree), "aggravated" assault and battery on a police officer (and that does not mean the cop was aggravated because junior took a swing at him), intimidation of a State witness, trafficking/manufacturing drugs (not "just" dealing) and a few others.

Let me stress again. I make every attempt to help a "youthful offender," but take a look at this list and tell me how many of these offenses, in your opinion, would never have occurred if "Officer Friendly" spoke to them at school. A scant few I would imagine. It all start's at home and it ends with us, but remember, we enforce the laws and you, the parents, must instill the values. Please don't let the heat of the moment, while you rush to the defense of your child, blind the real issue of why your child is here.

This is fairly recent, and very timely, so I'll drive on just a bit further.

I told you of arresting a kid several times, in a relatively short period of time, and he winds up back at home before I've finished with my initial report. Well, that's no big surprise. This kid never hit a cop that I know of, regardless of the crime that he was caught at, yet he was well on his way to making a name for himself (that usually means taking on the heat).

I always thought of this kid to be just that, a kid. I've arrested his mom several times, always strung out and, to this day, she wouldn't recognize me if I said who I was.

We constantly heard his name, of fugitives hiding in his mom's house (like she'd know), we've even taken fugitives from that house while she was there, but she could care less. Eventually, his name on the streets of Tulsa (he didn't start fires in his own back yard) earned him a gang name belonging to the developer of the sub-division where he lived. I'll not give respect to the gang by saying the name, but, that's how it started (food for thought in your "quiet" little area with an unruly little one).

To end this quickly, without giving credit to what he did, he crashed just south of our city limits and his spine shot through his skull. We had no idea what had started.

At his funeral, not only did the rival "gangs" arrive to show respect, but, every gang task force member within a majority of the state was there to film all those in attendance. It was then that we realized that this little pest of the past, the same one I'd arrested many times as a "kid," had grown to almost legendary status in the gang crime world.

I'm not giving his actions credit nor his life respect. I'm telling everyone that reads this book that it is happening, everywhere, and no pleasant little city or town is immune. If you watch the news tonight and hear of gang violence, and think how nice it is to live where none of that exists, do me a favor. Ask your local cop and he'll open your eyes. That's not said to scare you, just to let you know it's here, now, in every metropolitan village that has a convenience store.

Please don't read these words and be afraid to venture out at night, or decide not to fill up the gas tank if a group of kids are by the gas pumps. Just be careful and, the next time you see the cops "harassing" all the kids that drive your quiet town at night, give them credit for maybe just stopping a future gang legend before he decides to quit going to school, to make a real name for himself.

There was a time when almost every juvenile offender of tomorrow brushed his teeth, put on pajamas, kissed his mother at night, and, when he said his prayers, he asked the Lord that he could sleep tight.

Folks, let me be blunt. The kids that commit the crimes we read about today are the same kids that we bought Tonka Toys and Beanie Babies for. If they go wrong, badly, we must, to a degree, take partial blame. Yes, we, as parents, could do everything right and our cherished child still chooses the wrong path, but, lets look back about 50 years.

In 1948, there were guns out there, drugs (though granted, not as prevalent and to such a varied assortment) and windows to break, cars to steal, elderly to rob. I guess I could scan the vintage newspapers but I imagine I'd have to read a bunch of issues before I would find the headlines telling of a massacre in our local school, and today, it's almost expected.

Maybe one word will solve the mystery. The woodshed. That was the dire destination for a child of the past that dared back-talk Mom or misbehave in school. No, I will never advocate the abuse of a child. However, abuse versus discipline, that's a huge difference.

I mentioned earlier that, as kids, my (our) generation would never, ever contemplate showing any level of disrespect for our parents, let alone the police. Well, to make the obvious clear, our parents wouldn't tolerate it.

Folks, every cop has seen it a zillion times. The kids tell their parents, whether obviously or being discreet, and somehow, the folks of today often don't see what would have been so obvious, and so unacceptable, a half a century ago.

Maybe we can blame technology for, at least partial, blame. A pager now replaces a time to be home and a cellular phone offers all kinds of outs if the child is really having a good time. Adults can use today's technology to succeed, just as a child can abuse technology to even further diminish our parental control.

I guess "us" folks of today have, unknowingly, started to lose the advantage (actually it's the parents of twenty years ago to blame, darn you, well, it gives me an out). Where our children used to obey without question they now attempt, without possibly the disrespect that is the end result, to grow up just a little bit too quickly.

Don't guess I can blame them, to a degree. Kids of today look 18 when they're 14. Many of our future ladies apply make-up at nine and many of our young men pierce things at 12, often paid for by the folks. I, being a short haired (that means close minded to many) kind of guy, have always been uncomfortable seeing a young man, of say 7 or 8, with a long (rat) tail, often of unique colors, walking right next to the folks that approve or, and paid for, their boy to sport that tail, or Mohawk, or gang numbers etched from scalp up, name it.

Come to think of it, in the days of old, I don't remember my grandpa telling me of boys with colored hair, or girls of 8 wearing make-up and hose, with noses pierced, eleven earrings and black lipstick not being a sign of troubles to come. Remember, in those days, our kids still had respect for anything older than we were. Any connection? Could be, and right under our non-pierced noses.

CHAPTER FIVE
A Cop's Home Life

Let me give you a prime example of where a cop's devotion lies, not just for family, but for the job. I'll get to a cop's home life in a second, or at least a quasi-typical day off, but this just happened and I think it sums it all up nicely (well, at least honestly).

Our agency has been experiencing some serious and much needed changes, which included promoting two new officers. We, the supervisors, met with a newly promoted operations commander and the chief. The sole intent was to confirm where our department was headed and how to address and implement this new philosophy to the troops. I arrived about three hours late because my wife had out-patient surgical stuff planned, so after the procedure, I got her comfortable and headed off to the meeting.

Well, I missed about half of the first day and spent the whole night holding a cold compress to her head and leading the way to the bathroom as she threw up. It was non-stop from 9:30am to 10:00pm and, despite my world-wide fame of having zero vomit tolerance, I hung tough without hurling, myself.

With the support of a co-worker to make a late night cigarette and milk run, we survived the night and, with little sleep, I got my cherished (ok, so she's spoiled) daughter to school, cleaned house and headed for the second day's meeting.

I'm there for about ninety minutes and, of course, the pager massages my side and, in a faint, hurting voice, my wife is again feeling the effects of the day before. Well, after I knew the medication had worn off and no food or water could have caused this bout of nausea, I excuse myself from the meeting (again) and head to the emergency room, at the direction of her surgeon.

Upon our arrival, and after she immediately lost what stomach juice and cell fluid she had left in her body, the surgeon explained why she was feeling as bad as she was and we eventually headed back home. Of what possible relation does this greatly shortened version of the last 36 hours have to do with this subject?

I'm glad you asked.

After getting her home, and praying that she would start feeling better, my thoughts (I've got to be honest) were constantly on the meeting that I was supposed to be attending. I knew my absence was a hindrance.

I was gently placing my wife in bed and wondering who could be with her while I fulfilled my duties. I was trying to be the best cop I could be, for my community (that's your family and mine).

If I knew then, what I know now, oh what a different cop I would've been, or would I? Yes, I can easily justify every hour spent away from the family, specifically the wife in the beginning, and convince myself that it was for her and someday their benefit. If I get promoted I bring home more money; thus, the family will be the better off for it. If I don't put in all those extra "free" hours, I don't succeed and we'll never have all things we want for our family.

Why do cops talk so much about watching TV on those rare moments at home? Personally, I have a television set in every room. The bigger the room, the bigger the TV. The answer to the question is two-fold. Primarily, it's for entertainment and a release from work related stuff. Secondly, when I dare watch TV on those rare moments of down time, the domestic argument soon to follow will lead each of us to separate rooms, with a TV in it, and no doubt a $68.00 divorce commercial placing the idea into my wife's head of hunting greener pastures with a bigger house and a checking account that doesn't use both red and black ink on your monthly statement.

I would have not obtained all that I have if I didn't put my job first. The law enforcement world has been very good to me, but it wouldn't have had I not neglected my wife. Bear in mind, it's hard to realize what you're doing at the time, especially if the powers that be are glowing in your accomplishments, since it reflects on them too. You are constantly reminded of the bright career that lies ahead. Put aside the woman that brought you to your knees, the one you've sworn to have and hold until death do we part, she's home alone, every single night.

The first "residence" we shared was a tiny apartment that her father paid for. I couldn't have supported her, let alone a family. Had it not been for our parents we'd probably not even be together today, let alone in the beginning. We wouldn't have had food to eat, a television to watch or anything that we now take for granted.

Another irony, is how huge, yet lonely, that tiny two-room apartment must have felt to my wife.

I've told you already that I've been blessed with many awards. I was blind to this for many years, but looking back I realize that only a handful of times did the woman that I love, that I supposedly did all this for, ever join me by my side at those banquets held in "my" honor. Usually, if I recall (I think I've tried to block out this stuff), we had an argument before the ceremonies and I went on my way, alone.

I accepted the awards, and not until we separated, almost ten years after we married, did I give her and our daughter their just credit, at least in the newspapers. Too little and too late maybe, but it was important to me that the public knew how much I appreciated her support, though I actually felt that she didn't support me enough. If anything, I wished she'd quit griping because I was gone so much.

You know what? I did what I had to do. I've told myself that so many times I almost believe it.

This time away from home and family extends further than just the department. Usually cops have to get part-time jobs, especially in the beginning. If you're working a part time job, you're obviously not home and giving your family the attention they deserve. If you're home, you are probably fighting about not having enough money to pay the phone bill, or the mortgage (if your one of the lucky ones that owns a home,) quarters for the washing machine, you name it.

If there is any bright light to the path you've chosen, if you're a new cop starting out, the awfully tough yet rewarding road does get better, but only if you're sincere. At least it has for me, and somehow, though we did once file, well, twice, I've never been divorced even in a state with a high divorce rate. I am certainly the exception.

Most of the old timers that I work with, short of one, have all been divorced—most more than once. Bankruptcy also is a venomous and common word. In fact, there are few difficulties associated with struggling that I can't place almost every cop in, at one time or another.

We were fortunate. When my wife and I once sought the services of a bankruptcy attorney, he told us we were actually in great shape. I give him "the look," knowing it's impossible for an attorney to respect financial hardships, but I was wrong. We had little debt to speak of, but we had even less money. Bankruptcy had sounded like an easy way to start over, but we'd be paying for that escape to this day and regretting it had we gone that route. We found a good man, a truthful man, and he didn't take advantage of our plight to pad his bank account.

A good cop hopefully utilizes discretion in giving "a break" to those that are deserving. After all, you are powerless to effect the outcome, short of lack of experience and a great "floorshow." This attorney had the ability to change our lives, for the worse, and make money to boot, a cop's money, at that. He talked us out of "our ticket to financial ruins," and I never knew what a justice he did. I wish I'd have thanked him properly at the time, had I only known.

I found early on that I, unknowingly, attempted to right "my cop wrong" by cleaning the house, a lot. I told myself that I wanted a clean place for my family and I became almost fanatical about every counter being spotless and the floor vacuumed clean. I think now that I was trying to make up for neglecting the family and I did so by attempting to make our apartment worthy of museum quality standards. The intent was good, but the one's that I love the most would much prefer a "less tidy home" and more attention placed on them, instead of the coffee table.

Let me tell you of another terrible injustice that I did, and at the time, I was taking such pride in doing it, patting myself on the back for being the perfect dad. I spoiled my precious daughter to likes that few cop's incomes could afford. At seven years old, she had her own TV, with cable (but Mom did block the bad ones), her own phone line complete with caller ID, more toys than we had storage rooms for and her least little wish was a given necessity in my eyes.

I didn't realize then, and to a degree still don't, how I supplemented my nightly absence with monetary idols and felt I was doing the right thing. Sure, any layman couch psychologist (cookie doctor for the cops reading this) can see I wanted her to grasp all the tangible things and associate my absence with those items, and bingo, I'm still at home, in a way.

Actually, the idea isn't all that off base. Even those "desk dwellers" that make ten times the money, wear expensive clothes, eat lunch "on the company" and never get their hands dirty, they also buy dandy little trinkets for their daughters, they just cost more and your at home to watch them enjoy your heartfelt gifts. It is a little easier though when you get to go home to your family at night, every night.

Your kids don't have to substitute your absence for the toys because you're home while they are playing with them. You get all the kudos while we, the bastards that screw up your driving record, and in many of your white collar eyes don't have the intellect to control the corporate life, we have to keep inventing new ways of telling ourselves that we are good parents.

Are we good parents? Yes. We show them that we "unconditionally" love them, we certainly afford them the basic necessities and we'll always listen to their problems. I almost said we'd always be there if they were hurt, or in need of a hug, but if that hurt or hug is required in the middle of the night, we're probably tending to the hurt of the other families we've sworn to serve and protect.

Are you getting the idea that being a good cop parent is equivalent to pushing dental floss up an escalator, in the mall, on the day after Thanksgiving, if judged by your (white-collar) peers? It is, but, never forget it's a wonderful thing that we do and if we ever forget how vital our absence from our family is, what is so important to so many, especially those of us that can't be home, just read the newspapers or watch the evening news.

I bet the first two pages of the paper or the first minute on TV will show us doing our job, and always away from the family we so cherish, but without our feelings ever being mentioned or considered. That's not fair, but, that's but one of the costly prices we pay for working the ultimate job.

If you think for one minute when I kiss my wife good-bye, or scratch my daughter's back when I loll her to sleep, that I remember it might be the last time I get to do that, you're right. I have no intention of allowing my widow to hear a 21 gun salute, nor do I indent my chief to place an American flag in my daughter's lap. I'll do everything I can to stop it–but a man on the run or someone's pissed off spouse at a domestic could make it all happen if I let my guard down.

The white collar worker doesn't feel that sickness behind a

mahogany desk. And I live with that every time I start my cruiser.

There's one reason that we don't have to hunt under the car seats for food money, and her name is Kelli (my wife). You want to talk about being tight with money? If cotton costs half a cent a yard my wife would lose sleep over buying a piss ant a wrestling jacket.

Though it frustrates me often, I've got to give her credit. She writes all the bills (doesn't trust me, don't blame her) and my sole duty is to find the stamps and dump them in that little blue box. That much I can handle.

To be honest, if I go to the store for a loaf of bread she's truly amazed if I can keep it under a hundred bucks. So I'm compulsive, shoot me. I live for every day, not twenty years from now.

One other word on my dear spouse of a decade. Being a nurse, she often removes her rings since she has to constantly put on latex rubber gloves to keep from bringing nasty things from the field to the home front. I took advantage of this to swipe her wedding band one night and wedge it onto my little finger. It's a constant reminder of the one who tolerates what I do and yet another reminder, to me, of why I'm not at home and the real reason that motivates my now expected absence.

An interesting footnote. As I type now, my wife just dropped me off, I took a vacation day and, naturally, we've all been passing around a virus. They're off to find Valentine's cards for our daughter's class party. I'm cleaning boots, polishing brass and picking the lint off a uniform. Why? Maybe in preparation for my shift tomorrow night? No. I've again volunteered to speak, this time at a neighborhood youngster's school, and before eight o'clock in the morning.

So, I must now get to sleep early (on a vacation day, remember), get my daughter to bed and then up early, all so I can have her at one school and zoom off to another.

By the way, to the $1,200 suits, this is not for compensation, at least not in dollars. My compensation is being asked to speak, maybe reaching a future cop or two and hopefully putting to rest, at least for a while, the negative exploits of our law enforcement families that graced the TV screens last night.

Just to help you with the math, I'll be in uniform at sunrise, for the next two days. It's just another day for me and, though I may get sleepy or grouchy at the house, I wouldn't have it any other way (short of the tiffs at home that is).

Well, time now for some real domestic enforcement (gotta switch the clothes from the washer to the dryer!).

CHAPTER SIX
The White Collar World

You know what would be fun. Why don't the cops change places with the well-to-do for a month. We'll shed the uniforms for $1,200 Italian suits and you lug around the weight of a gun belt, and more importantly, the weight of being ultimately responsible. We'll trade sitting in a car seat for a high back leather chair and a window view of downtown. If we make a mistake, we'll just push the backspace key or call someone to audit our errors and blame the problem on somebody down the line. If we oversleep then we call the office and say we had a business engagement or worked late. Our productivity will be evaluated by the Board of Directors, which is far better than a shooting review board. Instead of asking for your driver's license and insurance we can ask for a wine list or ponder what our tee time is.

Those that don't understand what a vast canyon of differences there is between what you (white collar folks) do, and what we do, and how little we respect each other, is like comparing a black hole to a gnat's ass. But, let's put our bank accounts and work schedules aside. Let's look where we're more similar than you might think.

We both work for a living. That's a good place to start, for there are few things I loathe more than an able person who would rather have us support them with our tax dollars (and it happens a lot more than you think). We both have expectations, and my bosses have uniforms but they also live in every house and apartment in our jurisdiction. We have to please them all.

Your uniform is a suit, but it is a uniform. Just like we can't wear jeans and a football jersey to the office, you can't either (short of some Fridays). In other words, the people you deal with on a daily and professional basis expect a certain appearance. Well, at least that's a start.

We also have deadlines, to a degree, and both are usually in a written text. One huge difference. Our misspelled words or incorrect numbers (statutes) result in a criminal being wrongly set free or the re-filing of countless documents to save the case. The white collar world can justify a typo. We can't.

You have an advantage that we don't. A corporation or conglomerate backs your report, usually with pretty charts and fancy graphs. We have only words, in black and white, and it's our name, and our reputation, that must stand trial. If we lose our credibility then we might as well turn in our badge and start over.

We don't have a peon to blame or a public relations firm to salvage our careers. Enough paper talk, let's drive on.

We both have fantasy expectations of how wonderful our careers will be. Something very, very important that I only recently realized. I thought of how much I wanted to do, how I would yearn to know what the best cop could ever hope to achieve, that was what I wanted and when I would know that I was a success. The important part, simply, was that at no time did I evaluate my success with money. How many in the corporate world can (or would) admit that?

I must stress something and be very clear, and I mean this with all that is me. I neither envy nor disapprove of a "white collar" worker that succeeds, if, and that's a big and sincere "if," they dare not judge us.

If you wanted to be a lawyer, a bank president, an accountant, whatever, and you fought to be the best you could be, then I'll support you whole-heartedly. I respect that, just as I respect a kid who always wanted to be a cop and determined that he would be the best cop to ever walk a beat if he only got the chance. But, If you lose sight along the way and fall into the trap of letting your credit limit dictate your motivation for doing what you do, then you've lost the game.

It's that simple, folks. When the almighty dollar becomes your biggest reason for doing what you do, you'd better take a huge breath and return to what brought you to where you are.

Now, let's talk about the most important part of our lives, or what should be, our family. The white collar world does have one drawback that most cops don't face. Travel. Though we travel occasionally, usually dependent on our department's budget, or the law enforcement job that you've chosen, and more importantly has chosen you, you travel routinely dependant on your given level of success.

For those of you that use this opportunity to cheat on your

spouses, close this book and go elsewhere. I hope I'm talking to professionals and if taking a plane trip means hunting for strange, you're not in my class. You've already lost track of why you are traveling and I'll not support your libido to justify your ego.

If anyone (other than a cop, hose-dragger, medic or doctor) has spent Christmas away from the family, due to their job, and felt that it was worth it, please explain it to me. Or better yet, explain it to your little ones. It's hard enough for me, but I can honestly say that my working when Santa's sleigh flies overhead is for a reason. When you tuck your kids in bed at night, I'm out there hoping that they really do sleep tight. I don't want a bed bug or a boogieman one coming near our future while I'm on the beat.

Another similarity is the pride, or unfortunately at times, the shame that our family holds for the careers we've chosen. Very seldom, with the exception of lawyers, do kids on the playground get hassled when the other children find out mommy or daddy is a "suit."

Be a cop's kid and you're either the popular or the ridiculed, depending on how the other kids' folks talk to them at night. Hopefully, it's positive and kids begin to trust us, even hope to see us or talk to us on the street. But, when parents get a ticket on the way home, or make that mistake of driving when they've had too much to drink, think about what the kids hear that night.

Please choose your words carefully, or even better, if you must vent, do so in private. Many times I've heard of kids that were afraid of the police because of an incident that happened to mommy or daddy, due in no fault of the police, but we take the blame when you're safely back at home.

Make no mistake, if you weren't treated fairly, and professionally, then there are recourses. However, if you were at fault, please don't let your embarrassment scar your kids' impressions of us. If you promise to lay blame where it truly belongs, I'll shut up.

I believe one bridge that separates terribly our understanding for each others jobs, or lack of respect for what we each do, is that we are ignorant of our respective jobs. Sure, we may have a basic idea of the general fundamentals, but, how to properly do a given job is truly only known by those that do it. If we could gather a dozen of the nation's finest in a board room, and a dozen of the world's most powerful CEO's, what a debate it would be. Though no meaningful conversation would result if cops were seated in uniform and the CEO's were taking notes with $200 pens.

Ok, scratch the boardroom. We all have to wear blue jeans, football jerseys, tennis shoes (same brand) and we meet by the lake. Not at a split-level lake house retreat, but in cheap tents and each of us finding wood for a campfire. Now let's talk and see how similar we really are. (Ok, scratch that tent noise, we'll split the condo.)

I'm sure I'd respect you more as a person, instead of an overpaid magnate and, just maybe, you'd realize that cops can not only think on their very own, but actually possess an intellect worthy of your attention. If anyone that fits this category is willing, I promise I'll round up some other cops and give it a shot...I dare you.

Really. No, really.

Let me tell you a program that we have where I work. You fill out a piece of paper saying you won't sue us if you get hurt (shot, stabbed, mangled, mauled, twisted, burned, spat on, lose an appendage, etc.), we complete a background check and, bingo, your in my police car, "trolling" the streets. Again, I challenge you. Put the Italian suit in the cleaners and give it a shot. I'll show what radios to use if I get in trouble, how the lights work, what to look for, you name it. Or just sit back and watch.

Your perception based on television and the movies might just change. If you already support the police, then I really want you riding with us, even if just for one night. We not only appreciate your support, we *have* to have it.

What a thrill it is for a subject I've stopped, whether he gets a ticket, a warning, or even goes to jail, to say, "I really thank you for doing a job I sure as hell wouldn't." For those that say it to get out of a ticket, sorry, I've read that book. For those that say it with sincerity, I'll still do my job, but you really have made my night. You re-light that fire that first flickered when we dreamed of being a cop. Those simple words really are worth more than gold. For those that have, I sincerely thank you.

Another common scene we deal with routinely is waking you up, usually in the middle of the night, to tell you your business was broken into or you child is at the station. You must realize that we take your business getting burglarized on our watch as a personal insult.

Please understand that you must help us by getting out of bed, meeting us at the scene and taking the time to tell us what's missing. If we catch the bad guy (and that is our goal), you probably must testify as well. Though we treat your property as if it was ours, *you're* the victim. Show up for court!

Don't get mad at us because it happened. If we had 500 businesses, and 20,000 homes, we would need 25,000 cops to ensure you're not violated. You have to realize it's three or four cops that are actually out there, watching every headlight and every early morning jogger, not to harass, but to hope we don't have to wake you up an hour later.

Allow me tell you of the many traffic stops I've made on the "white-collar, well-to-do." Without exception, you either treat us with the utmost of respect or you make it quite obvious that this unscheduled interruption of your day is as inconvenient as it is *our fault.* As a rule, I can tell you that the reason for the "inconvenience" was either speed or alcohol related, and we neither pressed your foot to the pedal nor poured any drinks down your throat.

Expensive cars have fast engines, couple that with a busy schedule and a cellular phone to distract your attention from the speedometer and, bingo, here we come. Do us all a favor. If you were speeding, we don't need to see a wad of bills protecting your license, nor will an alligator wallet with gold cards impress the majority of us, though it can be effective on a new cop still afraid to rock the boat, especially in a small town.

I remember stopping a gentleman in a newer model Mercedes, accompanied by his diamond studded, mink warmed wife as he was weaving visibly down the street. When I made contact with him I could smell the odor of alcohol (he possessed the physical identifiers consistent with the consumption of alcoholic beverages–that was for the benefit of the DUI attorneys) and he couldn't have been more pleasant. He admitted to having "just a couple of social drinks," thanked me for my concern and asked if he could leave.

I'll admit it now, at that early part of my career, I was intimidated. I knew that if I pursued the matter, and if he wasn't intoxicated by legal definitions, I'd have hell to pay.

As he drove off, my backing officer saw that he was still weaving and, as the shift went on, I couldn't get the fact that I let him go out of my mind. Granted, he wasn't a "fall downer," but, he was "a keeper." *And he could have killed.*

If that same stop would have occurred a few years later, he'd have been going with me, and his wife for public intoxication (that's a book on its own so I won't even go there now).

I remember my chief of police at the time asking me to work over for a few weeks, during the morning school zone hours. At the beginning of a new school year, in an attempt to re-familiarize the public to the yellow flashing lights and the blue haired ladies with portable stop signs and orange vests, we try to be very visible.

Never having been one to be shy with traffic enforcement, I jumped at the opportunity to save our future from harm and even bring home a little overtime pay, maybe even pay a whole phone bill for a change.

On the first day, I stopped two that really tell it all. One was not only a school teacher, but in an administrative position (and a nice suit) he was actually the one that had requested the extra enforcement. If I recall, he was traveling 45-mph in the 20-mph zone.

At first it was embarrassment, then the defense mechanisms, that let his mouth overload his "assctions." He knew this was one he'd draw serious heat for and, though he almost talked himself into jail, he signed the ticket then immediately hit his office phone and called anyone who was anyone, trying in vain to make it all go away (and no, I refused to void the ticket).

The second, and this hurt, was a well-known pastor at one of our largest churches. He was doing 48-mph and couldn't have been a bigger jerk. He all but threatened me with the rapture, sloppily scribbled a fancy "x" on the dotted line, threw his ticket in the floorboard and sped off, too fast. As the grass and gravel flew onto my patrol car, with tires crying, I called for a supervisor as I started to stop him again. I doubted seriously that his license had been suspended in the 30 seconds since I last checked so, when I approached his car and he started to open his door, in disgust, I saved him the trouble of asking for my boss and told him to stay in his car.

What a change when the boss showed up. The preacher was beyond cordial, stated that I had radared the wrong car and accidentally stopped him, though he respected the job we had to do. He added that the loose shoulder made his tires slip and he was offended that I would even insinuate that he would have "sped off like a criminal," shaking his head in utter disbelief.

He concludes with a quasi-sincere statement that we'll be in his prayers and he professionally signs the ticket, thanks me with his hand outstretched and ever so gingerly putters on his way. At least he knows what happened and, though my boss knew something was up, his acting job was able to plant the seed of concern in the eyes of the administration at least for a moment.

As the years passed, I was fully supported by the administration, but the performance that day was worthy of an Oscar, and, he succeeded in really hitting my button, and he knew it.

I will thank him for this much. He taught me a great lesson, I learned what couldn't be taught in a classroom from the experience and, not only did it make me a better cop, it would, in the future, make me a better field supervisor. Come to think of it Reverend, thanks.

We recently went through a period where thieves were isolating on homes of the "well-to-do" that left the garage doors open at night. You leave available for the bad guys your cars (often with keys in the ignition), your golf clubs, power tools, anything that can be grabbed or started is fair game.

Our shift began waking folks up, just to say their garage door was open and that the bad guys are looking for just such an invitation. Some were overwhelmed that we cared that much. Others were downright pissed off.

I had one thank me to the point I actually had to excuse myself to resume patrolling. The next person made it quite clear it was his home, his property and he'd leave his car running all night if he wanted to and told me to mind my own business. I shook my head and went on doing my job knowing that if I hadn't gotten the guy up that he would have been complaining the next morning that he had been victimized and asking why the hell weren't we doing our job.

Many in uniform would be tempted to say, "Fine, your wish is my command but don't come crying to me, at least we tried." Like I said earlier, you can't please them all and you'll go nuts trying, but, when you let it get to you, you'd better take another real deep breath or get your paycheck elsewhere.

My goal is not to impress you, but to just maybe open your eyes.

I have been critical, possibly too much so at times, but please read between the lines. Does any "white collar" reading this book care so much about what they do that they work late, for no compensation (takes out the salaried and CEO's) just so your work product is the best it can be? Zero money on the bottom line here, just work product based simply on its own merits. No extra profit. No commission for lowering the crime rate. Our work product goes far deeper than landing that big account that will move you up two floors, to an office with more windows and a better view of the park and not the parking lot.

When you go to work tomorrow, don't think about your office, or your suit, or even what's on the lunch menu. When you sit behind your Mahogany desk, and send for that first cup of coffee, think about what you really can do for the people you work for. Do the very best you can, with no financial motivation, and I'll bet you'll surprise yourself. Or just maybe you'll remember back to when you applied for that job and you said what a valuable asset you would be if only given the chance.

To close on this area, I do wish you well and hope that you prosper beyond even your wildest dreams. I hope you don't have to meet us in an unfavorable light and you have the blessing of seeing every play and ball game and science fair your kids ever take part in.

The only football or basketball game I see is when I'm away from my family and working security. You deserve to succeed, if your success is internal and you can sleep at night, comfortably, knowing that you did the best you could, for your family. We'll be driving around your neighborhood to guarantee that much needed night's rest, doing the best we can at our job.

CHAPTER SEVEN
Shift Change

Well, the sun is going down and it's time to get ready for work. First, and this is important, you've gotta look perfect. The dry cleaner hopefully has every crease pressed to a fine, clean line and the brass accouterments must shine as if they were in Tiffany's window. Your boots must reflect a mirror shine (forget about the creeks and muddy backyards you were in last night) and if you can't floss your teeth in your brass buckle then get ready to greet the carpet. Make sure your gun barrel has no dust, your leather is shined and your wit is sharper than a Ginsu knife. And we haven't even made to our mobile office, our cherished cruiser.

Primarily, it must be free of dirt, dust, mud, bird dinners and squirrel farts. Your tires must glimmer and your dashboard should be as sterile as a surgeon's scalpel. You must ensure your radios work, your siren makes the dogs bark and your overhead lights wake up the citizens we've sworn to protect (so they can complain about it later.)

All kidding aside, you *must* know exactly what your car can do. Your next attempt at a traffic stop might well end up in another city. I'll get into pursuits later, and it's a good chapter, but let's walk first.

You must make sure that every piece of equipment is operational. That's lawsuit preventative maintenance folks, and, you talk about passing the buck down the line, this is where it's gonna start (remember the inspection sticker).

Before we fire up that *marked machine of death* (defense lawyer thinking), we must ensure the paint hasn't been scratched with car keys and the tires aren't resting on the rims. I've had it all, and I'm nice to just about everybody. My windows have been smashed, my tires have been slashed and I often see dried spit on either the hood or the windshield.

I can't tell you how many beer cans I've removed from the light bar or how many whiskey/beer bottles were tucked underneath a wheel, hoping I wouldn't see them as I started my night. I've had nasty reminders of what a lousy group we are left on the windshield wiper, the antennas bent to resemble those of insects and everything from fruit to rocks shoved in the tail pipe.

Amazingly, we must somehow take it in stride and still personify excellence and caring from the first to the last citizen we'll meet this night. It's part of the job and you can't take it personal. In a way, it's a gift. The bestower of these gifts are too much the coward to do anything to our face, but it's a reminder to be on guard for those that would prefer to see *us* hurt, and not our cars. In a way, your cowardly actions, often the result of a beer-induced moment of machismo (in your mind) may have given us that edge we need to stay healthy. Thanks.

Well, our appearance is worthy of a guard at Buckingham Palace and our patrol sleds are ready for parade duty. We call the station to let them know we are in our unit and ready to roll, head to the gas pumps just in case the bad guys wanna run early and then it's off to the station to get briefed on what our fellow brothers and sisters just endured.

We listen intently to the pass on, get Intel (intelligence) reports on problem areas and out we go, into the night. Many fear the darkness but we're just waking up and actually feel uncomfortable when the moon falls and that blindingly bright sun gets its first cup of coffee.

You never really know what to expect on the street. It might be a slow night or calls may be backed up and you scramble to the hot ones, prioritize the lukewarm ones and the cold calls may go ignored for a while, guaranteeing another complaint from the public left waiting. Their call might be a trivial matter to us, but it's darn vital to them and they just don't understand that somewhere else in the city a life might be at stake. We can justify that complaint but we've lost the faith of a citizen, which is a bloodletting loss. The next time they see us we will be casually patrolling, obviously able to take that trivial call now, and they'll forever wonder if we were just driving in circles when they last summoned for our response.

Well, our first course of action is a hot cup of coffee. We greet the convenience store attendants we'll be watching all night, take a leak and out we go. Time to look for the garage doors, the Popeye's (cars with a headlight out), the weavers, the hoopti-mobiles, the Mario Andretti wannabes and, my personal favorite, to catch the drunks.

I'll let you in on a piece of advice. Guys, if it's after midnight and I see two or more cowboy hats I know a cold beer is about to get shoved underneath the seat as I pass. Your biggest hope is that we're going opposite directions so you can send them beer cans launching when I make that oh so dreaded turn to head for your tail-lights.

How about this for a changing times. Sometimes while on patrol I'd see kids throwing a football, baseball or Frisbee and I'd slow down, roll down my window and put my hands out. With the catch of one little object I've left a positive impression that will never fade. I recently heard of folks that would take advantage of even that simple a gesture intended only to let the public know we're human.

It happened in Milwaukee and those that want to hurt others, especially them dogs in uniform (the po-po's), found yet another way to make us not want to even join a game of catch. They make a cut in a tennis ball, fill it with a combination of "strike all" match heads and BB's, buckshot, nails, etc, and re-seal it with duct tape. When the ball is thrown against an object, the compression of the rubber allows the match heads to ignite. The result is a gaseous chain reaction that causes the ball to explode, expelling whatever they filled it with to expel the shrapnel. The inventors of this fine device were, of course, a gang (the Gangster's Disciples, so I've read) and I seriously doubt they thought about it during recess.

They're really out there folks, bunches of them and I pray it's just us simple minded, silent barristers of street justice that have to deal with them on the street. Odds are, the good folks we live to protect will only see them on the TV at night. If you do, look who's standing next to them, trying to ensure you only see them on TV.

You want to know a personal, routine frustrator. The paper delivery folks. They drive all over the road, usually wrap papers while their driving and often ignore those octagonal distractions as well as the speed limit signs.

I've written them tickets, but usually only when really flagrant violations occur because I do respect the fact they drive all night, but they always have an attitude when they see the ticket book and don't get to fly away with their usual warning. I wrote one carrier for driving 68mph in a 35-mph zone.

He couldn't have been a bigger ass and he had me hoping he wouldn't sign the ticket but he knew he was pushing it and not a lot of papers will reach their doorsteps if he's in jail. In other words, he'd be on the receiving end of the complaints. Hard to tell your boss the papers didn't make it because you were caught going 33mph over the speed limit and you got jailed for having an attitude (thought no doubt those dogs in blue were the jerks). Enough about that but it is a common occurrence.

The beauty, and beast, of field patrol is having full knowledge that you have absolutely no idea of what's next. I remember starting out a shift and being requested to respond to a possible accident on a dark road just out of our jurisdiction. For those unfamiliar with law enforcement, when an adjoining agency requests your immediate assistance, you're immediately deputized for that jurisdiction, for that particular call of service (as long as you have a mutual-aid agreement).

I arrive at the scene, which was a possible vehicle accident/ trouble unknown, and what I saw was truly unique. A young man had driven off the road, got stuck in the ditch and a good Samaritan, with a four wheel drive, stopped to help him out. Well, as it turns out, the Samaritan hooks a chain up to the car, pulls him out, and as they were in the process of unhooking the tow chain, here comes Mr. Drunk Driver. The young man that got stuck was in the process of unhooking the chain from the bumper and, while expecting the oncoming motorist to stop, he just watches the car get closer and closer. The car crashes into the rear of his vehicle and slams the two other cars together with the young man in the middle. The bumpers catch the young man just above the knees.

The impact takes the legs away (I'm all too familiar with this scene) and I remember two things very, very clearly. First, he displayed absolutely no sign of pain (that's called shock, I mean real shock, not like the shock of losing you're breath when a smart ass scares you). Secondly, I looked up inside his leg, and saw what seemed like a huge, empty cavern. There were little pieces of bone, surpassingly not much blood loss (at first), and I literally saw his artery. I'll also never forget that when the medics got to the scene, with an air ambulance following, they grabbed a leg and put it in "mass pants."

It was initially pointed the right way, as in pointing up since he was on a gurney, but, just before closing the ambulance door, the leg "part" slid around and was now pointing at the ground. I found out later, by emergency room veterans, that I had arrived soon enough that the impact "pinched" the artery, which was a temporary natural suture and then the blood built up and then the geyser erupted (and I mean everywhere).

It's a common thought among those that we protect that cops are cold-hearted from what they've seen. To a degree, that is true. We develop a thick skin for survival's sake, yours and ours. But we pay for it sooner or later. We're human and we hurt too.

How would any of us feel if a policeman shows up at the scene of an incident, looks at the blood and body parts and then begins crying and has to go sit on the curb or leave the area? No question, our faith in their ability would be gone. Not just that cop, but every cop you'll ever see for the rest of your life, be it on your quiet street or the movie screen. How many have ever seen an officer cry at a scene? Now, think about the countless times we've seen or heard of a violent situation, or been involved in one, yet the police maintained their composure.

That's where you hopefully begin to understand the make-up of what it takes to be a cop. We do feel, we do care and we do hurt, we just don't allow you to lose faith in our profession. It's vital that you have faith in us and it's even more vital, for every single person that will ever see a badge that you know we can unconditionally control any situation that we encounter. We will cover the only exception to this rule, we'll bury a cop later in this book.

By the way, we do cry, at times, but just not at the scene. If a broken child dies in our arms, or we try to save a family member's life, unsuccessfully, it will hit us, just most likely not at the scene. Adrenaline is a unique substance the body produces for dramatic times, and thank the good Lord, he gives cops an over-abundance. But he allows us to get home or to the station before he allows our emotions to overtake us. The family of a cop, they don't see the tears, just the pain and resentment. It's really not fair to them, but that's the law enforcement life, at it hits hardest at the family core. Maybe that's why we try to be gentle when we're out of uniform and we try to help with the "family" chores. Yes, it is guilt, but it stems from pride, and that combination of emotions, my friends, would have Sigmund himself seeking the Yellow Pages for a family counselor.

You want to know how to find an open door every night on patrol and show your bosses you're out shaking doorknobs? Go to the nearest church. They've all got 600 doors and at least one is open and nothing, I mean nothing, has more little rooms and hallways than a church.

I remember, while a campus cop, that I saw several young guys hop a fence, into a huge warehouse area and I was hot on their trail. I crossed the fence, headed where I last saw them and the search is on. I find an open door, initiate a building search and, not knowing if they're armed or not, my gun is out.

I clear room after room until, as I sporadically shine my flashlight, as the small circle of light scans one room I spot something in the corner. I almost pull the trigger on a bad guy, hiding amongst the boxes. It takes a slight amount of trigger pull to end a life or forever change a career and I was close, very close.

My bad guy, as it turned out, was a life-sized figure of Jesus with his hands clutched in prayer by his chest. Tell me I would ever live that one down. I've heard of cops shooting everything from vacuum cleaners to mirrors on the backside of a door, but, if I ever have a shooting situation that isn't a life or death matter, I really don't want Jesus involved, at least if he's not on my side.

I'm a religious person, though I keep it to myself, but I'll be darned if I want to shoot Jesus in a Nativity scene and see that played back on the big screen at the Pearly Gates. No doubt St. Peter has seen it all but he'd surely have the all trumpets blowing on that one when I'm ready to enter.

By the way, while on the subject, I got a Mother's Nature fact that might help you some day. If the storm clouds are swelling, and the lighting is crackling, and the winds are a howling, I can save you. Run to the garage, straight to the golf bag and grab your one iron. A two iron will do if that's all you got. Now save your family and crawl to the roof, balance yourself on the highest chimney brick and point that club straight at the loudest and brightest that Mom Nature has to offer. You've saved the family for another day! (Even the good Lord can't hit a one iron.)

One of the biggest drawbacks of the midnight shift is food. If you patrol a city of less than 15,000 - 20,000 you either bring food from the house or browse through the soy burgers and nuke them at a convenience store. At that, the odds of actually finishing you meal uninterrupted are highly unlikely anyway. A cop gets a real intelligent stomach, often laden with ulcers, but you know within about the three bites how long that pre-fab sandwich has been in the cooler.

It's amazing how many complaints are received, on patrol officers, for simply following a car. I handle complaints, often on myself, because the citizen felt wrongly treated by being dogged from the minute they enter the city limits until they make it to the driveway.

We don't know if you've been drinking without following you for a while, nor do we know if you're casing one of our neighborhoods until we observe your actions and get a return on your license tag. Our intent is not to harass, but to protect. I promise you this and know it to be a fact, many people with criminal intent will not enter our city because they know, on the street, that they'll get followed, hounded if you will, as soon as they drive into our city limits.

We have reduced crime, saving you the torment of being a statistic, by following every car we can. If you didn't get stopped, and most won't, please be happy that we do follow every car. It is for a reason other than we "just can" that we line up at the city boundaries much like a cab driver waiting for a fare. It's easier for cabbies though, for rarely do the criminals hail us down. It does, however, occur.

I was on patrol one night when a gentleman waved me over, obviously distressed. He said, quite simply, that he was being chased by "a big guy that's trying to kill me." I scan the horizon in search of Bigfoot and, as a really big guy approaches, my bad guy wants to confess to breaking into his home. I instruct the good old boy to chill, handcuff the now bad guy and I've just gotten credit for the arrest of a burglar. Most obviously aren't that easy, but it does happen. Fortunately, most bad guys are not applicants to Harvard.

Another example, and I love this one, tells of the smarts that aid, or often destroy, the desires of wanna-be bad guys. A couple (man and woman, not sure what city) decide to rob a convenience store and, with minimal forethought, they drive about 20 miles from home. Upon entering the store they wait for a customer to leave, both pull handguns and each point a gun at the two attendants. The male forces one attendant to the office, to empty the safe, while the female stays at the counter with the other attendant.

The attendant, who certainly earned my respect, tells the lady robber of a contest that's being held and she, the bad girl, not only listens intently but fills out the form, complete with their actual address and home phone number. When the partner surfaces from the office, with bounty in hand, they flee into the night. It takes less than an hour for a special operations team to surround the house, announce that they want to say hi, and, both surrender. She actually wrote their address, phone number, even driver's license information.

This scenario, though unique, is not that uncommon. We've all seen many times how police departments hold sting operations, offering TV's, vacations, cruises, etc, to persons with outstanding arrest warrants, and of course, they show up. Personally, if I was a wanted person, I'd be laying so low that I could walk under a milk-bearing pregnant snake's udder.

The downfall of most criminals, and to a much lesser degree all of us, is greed. A "what can I get" mentality. If they aren't willing to earn it, by working, then they'll either steal it or take advantage of someone else's misfortune. Criminals steal to obtain a good lifestyle. If not to decorate their homes, or to sell their ill-gotten booty for drug money, it's to have possessions that can make them feel successful.

Ironically, many crooks steal to afford their spouses, or kids, the things that they, the provider, should provide, right motivation but certainly the wrong method. I promise you that, while stealing from others, and often justifiably in their minds, to have such an act perpetrated to their own families would warrant emotions similar to that of a rape victim. In no way could one be more violated, yet, their actions were for a reason, unless their on the receiving end of the easy way out.

So sue me, I strayed onto another story. Let's get back to the streets.

The actual productivity of a given street officer is usually based on his or her own level of motivation. Many police administrators have told me through the years that you need all kinds. From the "stallions" that don't even want to take food breaks for fear of missing an opportunity to enforce violations to the "slugs" that limit their contacts to the flagrant acts committed right in front of them.

I used to think that all stallions would be the best, but as an administrator, I guess I could see both sides, kind of a balance of powers. All stallions might slow the traffic but surely the business and residential areas would suffer, hoping that is, that the slugs are working those areas while the stallions are wearing out their overhead light bulbs. That's where supervisors play their biggest roles.

Being an effective police patrol supervisor is a very challenging feat, if done correctly. If your too easy on the troops you've failed to motivate and if you're too much the tyrant your troops dread coming to work.

I've worked for all types, and though I prefer discipline to a ghost supervisor, absolute power corrupts if not kept in check and motivated by experience and personal devotion, not just to the citizens but to the administration of the department. I will say, from experience, that a disciplinarian results in immaculate appearances and early to work, late to leave field troops.

It is vital however, if you fit into the latter category, that you occasionally allow the troops to see the human side, not just a tyrant with expected robotic actions. Above all, never preach if you don't practice, and live, your sermon. No one commands less respect than a supervisor that mandates one thing but, given his tenure and been there, done that attitude, doesn't follow his own ground rules.

More food for thought for every police supervisor that hasn't allowed his/her brain cells to selectively forget the days of the academy.

Another really tough aspect of serving your communities on the "hoot" shift is being fresh and prepared. Every aspect of life, short of the criminal element and shift work, perform their daily duties during the normal business hours and we must accommodate our basic necessities with this established norm. Every bill we pay, every loan we take, anything associated with our family, and all must be attempted prior to the arrival of our cherished moon. The phone always rings when you're sound asleep and few knock on the door when you're awake.

Your basic desire to always be available eliminates your wish to turn the ringer off, ignore the doorbell or take the batteries out of your pager. If you're a real productive officer that means a lot of court and, of course, that means staying in uniform, waiting forever for the docket to bear your name and yearning for those rare down times you get to visit with your pillow. Sleep is a vital but rare commodity and don't forget, we must be well rested before we ever strap on our gun belt. Good luck.

Throw in part time jobs, adjusting your sleep on days off to make up for neglecting your spouse and your body's internal clock never knows when to sleep. Enough already, you get the point.

Here's a unique topic, waving. While on patrol I must wave a hundred times, and that's if I'm covering a shift that has that nasty, blinding sun trying to test my patience. Often, I wave before the car passing me does and they either think they've done something wrong or it was a mistaken identity.

Much of this most simplest of public relations depends on the area that given driver called home. Big cities expect a team of heavily armed soldiers to emerge from a heavily window tinted van and small cities expect that sign to indicate you'll be late for dinner.

Yes, I have had people pull over because I waved my hand as a sincere salutation, but had to circle the block to tell them they hadn't committed a violation and I was just saying hi. That's an ugly and far step from the common decency that was expected from the "cop on the beat." It's truly sad how a simple gesture of care is nowadays associated with one having done wrong. Does that give you an idea of how far crime has become common place and "good cops" are a thing from the western past? Truly sad.

You know the ones that I wave to that don't take offense to this action? The elderly, or the very young. They actually love to wave back and now I know why. When they were kids there was a cop on the beat and every cop that made the TV's and newspapers hadn't been charged with a crime or, like me as a child, every cop was good. I still get one of my best thrills at waving back, telling that select group, or any other, that we are still here, we do still care and yes, you're why we circled the block.

One of my favorite times to patrol, though a traffic nightmare, is Halloween. Our administration even provides bags of candy so we're prepared for all the ghosts and goblins. Still, if you pull to the side and beckon the little ones over, with the intent of sabotaging their dental co-pay, many still begin the conversation with, "What did I do?" You then extend a candy bar, they give a skeptical "thanks" and off they go. Hey, as long as it helped to bridge even a faint belief that we still care, I'm satisfied.

The main drawback, on Halloween, is the crackling of our police radio. The fear that every cop knows can, and does happen, is the vehicle vs. pedestrian accident. Nothing, but nothing, brings your gut to the basement more than a call of a child that's been hit by a car. You immediately think the worst. Severed legs, heads split open, arm or leg bones poking out of the skin, name it, I've seen it and I always will hate it. At least you can tell an adult to calm down.

A child, with excruciating pain and the belief their young life is over by virtue of the blood dripping from their innocent bodies, that's a chore. Add Mom screaming in the background, which only compounds their fears and it makes for a really bad scene.

Everyone reading this book has most likely dealt with such a scene at least one or twice in their lives. Try doing it every single time you put on a uniform, or at least living with the prospect that it can happen. That's but one reason I harbor so much respect for ambulance crews. They don't draw a decent salary, like the doctors that (after residency) have such a comfortable lifestyle, though the hours do stink. The "field doctors" make in a year what the surgeons will make in a week, or a good night given their level of expertise, but they actually see far worse than the big money health care professionals do.

The paramedics/EMT's see the raw, natural, un-sterilized pain in its truest form. They put bones close to where they should be, stop the bleeding, start the medications and clean em' up, all before the emergency room doors open. They get little of the praise if the victim survives and all the blame if they don't. To any of those public safety professionals that are with me now, at least in spirit, you have my utmost respect and admiration. After all, you're the ones that see our uniforms covered with blood and tiny holes in the material that sent the bad guy's bullets into our flesh, while you want nothing more than to see us back in our cruisers, patrolling your homes while you sleep. Again, thanks for a job very well done.

While I'm thinking about it, let's talk for a sec about being on the receiving end of a traffic ticket. Odds are, and I know as much as it sickens me that not all stops are deserved, you most likely committed the violation that you were alleged to have committed. We expect for you to hope, or often plead, for leniency. That usually depends on either the flagrancy of the violation or the discretion of the officer. On a highway, being fifteen or twenty miles an hour over the posted limit, though illegal, isn't in the same category as doing the same where our kids ride their bikes and roller-blade. That's common sense, I hope.

That's but one reason we ask for a driver's license. Sure, we want to know who you are, if you're wanted for a crime (yea, like you'd have your real name on that license, and give it to us) but we really need to check that license for your driving history.

Personally, I hate to ruin a spotless driving record and I love few things more than to add to the list of offenses of an offender that could care less. If we say have a good day, after "giving" you a citation, we'll get a complaint. If we give you a ticket, say sign here, give you your copy and then just turn and walk away, we get a complaint. We are not either friendly enough or we mocked the situation by saying, "Have a nice day." And please remember this, if nothing else. Yes, you pay our salaries and yes, we do have better things to do. But, this is our job and most importantly, we did not ask you to commit the violation we swore our oath on, to enforce, that you committed.

For the cops and future cops reading this, I'll never write better words than what follows. If you enforce the laws out of a desire to do you job as well as you can, and always maintain professionalism and treat every offender with respect, not for what they did but for whom we serve, you'll do well. If that badge rules your decisions just because you can, and no thought process goes into your enforcement actions, don't plan on a career that will make your kids on the playground proud of saying, "My daddy's a cop."

I said I'd talk about "Mo" again and this is a good place. We were at the station, only three of us on duty and I'd arrested an early drunk driver (about 5 or 6ish in the evening). Neither I nor Mo was certified to run the breath test and, while the other officer was administering the test, a fight call is broadcast.

Well, it's just me and the Mo-man, but hell we can handle anything. It's an older part of town and, sure enough, there's three brothers "just scrappin" on the front lawn. The smallest one would field dress out at about 265 and, well, they just got bigger. Each wore the same clothing, specifically coveralls (usually only one side attached), no tee shirt, each had a beard and between them they didn't have enough teeth to make a Jack-o-lantern.

Anyway, here we are. We tell them to chill, get them separated, think the situation is calmed down and then (my fault, I didn't see it coming) my glasses fly off my face and my jawbone tingles. Yes, I got clocked and the fight is on. For those that don't "routinely" get into fights, a two or three minute fight will test the utmost of your endurance. I'll go to the end then start back. It was twelve minutes before the last was handcuffed. Not put in the back of my car, just handcuffed.

When we finally handcuff the one that destroyed my now departmentally owned glasses, he was on his stomach with me and Mo at either side and, with both of us being smokers, we're hunting desperately for clean air. We look up and, the biggest one (Jack) is steaming full force at Mo, who's on his knees, with his (the bad guy's) arms tightly straightened and his palms together. He clocks Mo straight in the middle of his face, Mo rocks backwards (fortunately he's shy of a neck, for it would have snapped and killed the mortal man) and little bursts of blood spew, in unison, from Mo's nostrils.

Well, we were agitated before, now we're both tired and pissed. In the following few minutes, well before the days of pepper spray and expandable batons, the black painted hickory "ugly sticks" go to work on anything that moves. We strike everything that's close to us and they, deliriously drunk, enjoyed nothing more than a "scrap" and were holding there own, for a while.

I will never forget while one is handcuffed and Mo is making a nightstick necklace on the biggest one's neck, he (bad guy #2) starts to twist my ankle. I don't mean he's applying pressure, I mean he's literally turning it like the hands on a clock. Skinny as I *was* then, I knew that when he released it we'd all be airborne. I guess Mo made the necklace fit just right for he let my ankle unwind and we went back to business.

Like I said, *twelve* minutes later, all are secured and it's at least another twelve minutes before me or Mo have enough breath to check on each other, much less attempt to advise dispatch we're ok or attempt a decent stadium wave or backyard high five. We were happy, but just a little to far gone to savor the victory, until what follows.

It was many hours before the processing and paper work were completed. While we sat at the end of the booking table, we couldn't wait to see our foe head to the back dock en route to the squad cars that would take them to a county lock-up (no municipal stuff involved when you fight us).

I will never forget this moment, nor will the Mo-man. If it took them twenty minutes it took them two days just to walk the thirty feet from the holding cells to the back door. Every step ached (but nothing, I imagine, like the next morning) and their nerves were still being saved by the booze.

I have never advocated using more force than what was necessary to handle a situation. In this situation, I think we could have used lethal force and been justified in a court of law, dependant of course, on how much the defense lawyer spent on his suit.

An interesting footnote. While I was working loss prevention at the grocery store, I saw the biggest brother and we addressed each other head on. He said, simply, "You look bigger sober, but I'll own up to it being my fault." I responded with shaking his outstretched hand (really carefully, this time) and he added, "Are you the one that popped my neck? Thanks, felt better ever since," and he just shook his head and went on pushing his cart, laughing to himself, yet out loud. He gave us his respect, but he just had to save face as well. That's fine with us. We can *all* live with that.

CHAPTER EIGHT
The Pursuit

It would take me a shelf full of books to fill you with the emotions that encompass every cell of a cop who's involved in a high-speed pursuit. There is nothing more enjoyable than the prospect of putting em' in cuffs afterwards nor anything more terrifying than the unforeseen potential pain and countless lawsuits that start the second we engage.

No question here. Every single police administrator, edged on by the city officials holding their jobs by the shorthairs, cringe at thought of the "P" word on the police radio. It filters from the city officials to the chief, from the chief to the captain/lieutenant, to the sergeant, to the corporal and finally, the troops, who are usually the ones that started it.

Got a bit of good news for a change. The United States Supreme Court, for a pleasant change, voted unanimously 9-0, in Lewis vs. Sacramento, "In the circumstances of a high-speed chase aimed at apprehending a suspected offender, where unforeseen circumstances demand an instant judgement on the part of an officer who feels the pulls of competing obligations, only a purpose to cause harm unrelated to the legitimate object of arrest will satisfy...Such cases with no intent to harm the suspects physically or to worsen their legal plight do not give rise to substantive due process liability." As simple as this sounds (at least in legal terms) this was a *huge* stroke on behalf of the good guys.

Why in the world would we not want our police officers to catch the bad guys? The following word I'm about to throw on you encompasses damn near every single action taken by police administrators and field supervisors. *Liability.* I wish we could spell it differently because no four letter word spoken in our darkest, nastiest alleys today creates such emotions, nor as much damage to our effectively doing police work.

In the Supreme Court ruling I just mentioned, the determining factor, in defining innocence or guilt, was whether the actions of the officer(s) "shocked the conscience." Well, and for those that have

83

been good enough to read thus far, shocking the conscience is as varied as dots on the census or as many $1,200 suits as you can fit into a given courthouse elevator. Don't get me wrong. In the event an Honorable Supreme Court Justice would do me the privilege of reading my words, I thank you, without exception Your Honor, and with that, this policeman rests.

A product was invented to stop fleeing cars, without gunshots or city owned vehicles, and it's called a stop stick. Basically, it's a long, skinny board with nail-like spikes that point upwards. When a vehicle crosses over the stop sticks, the spikes imbed in the tires and the bad guy slowly rolls to a stop. By the way, in case you didn't know, the appellate courts outlawed actually blocking a road, in a *roadblock*. You must allow them an avenue of escape, which, certainly takes away from the initial concept of a roadblock, or, blocking a road. Since we can't block roads (on a *roadblock*), and we get sued if we shoot out the tires, along came the stop sticks.

Let me read an account of a pursuit, that also involves about every chapter of this book, inclusive of Juvenile Crime, The Drunk Driver, The Pursuit, The Law, To Bury A Cop, etc.

On May 29, 1996, shortly after midnight, an Orange County deputy sheriff died of multiple injuries suffered when a stolen vehicle being driven through a police roadblock struck him. Attempting to establish a *roadblock* on the roadway ahead of the pursuit, the 37-year-old victim deputy, with less than 2 years on the job, was placing stop sticks on the roadway.

Allegedly, the driver of the pickup, operating the vehicle under the influence of alcohol, ran the roadblock, struck the deputy, and continued fleeing. Pursuing deputies fired at the truck, striking the driver several times until he lost control and crashed the truck. The 18-year-old suspect was hospitalized in critical condition, paralyzed from the waist down. He was charged with *second* degree murder. I guess it wasn't worthy of first degree murder since it wasn't, in the eyes of the court and a $1,200 suit, pre-meditated.

The cop is dead, trying to protect you, and with a new widow and fatherless children on the books, and yet another name etched on the Law Enforcement Officer's Memorial Wall, the suspect will be free in a relatively short time, if even convicted.

If they run, and we catch them, with nobody getting hurt, then we get a pat on the back. If they get away, or somebody gets hurt, or any of the most minute of infinite problems occur, it's dribble down time.

It starts with the lawsuits, dribbles down to the city administrators, then the police chief, the assistant chief, the major(s), the captain(s), the lieutenant(s), the sergeant(s), the corporal(s), then finally, the lonely street cop. The one that started all this mess. All in the relentless pursuit of the bad guy. After all, good folks don't run from the police, and our job, after all, is to catch the bad guy, isn't it? Now it gets ugly so fasten your seat belt.

Few people in street police supervisory roles, short of a field Sgt. or Lt. that hasn't forgotten where he/she came from (and hopefully myself) and a handful of others will support unconditionally one of the troops under their supervision for chasing a bad guy if things go to hell.

If we let them go that means getting called off by a higher-ranking supervisor, and the bad guy kills somebody, who's really to blame? If they don't kill someone in their flight from justice then they're free to harm others until somebody with the nards to do the job sees they get caught. I bet if liability meant allowing an offender to just run away, so that we don't get sued, then we could return to the days of true law enforcement.

My desire is not to lay blame, but to solve the problem. That takes the lawmakers establishing severe penalties for fleeing from cops and laws that support our desired end result of finishing our job. It may be a scared teenager behind the wheel, out after curfew and with a can of beer between his legs, or, it could be Timothy McVeigh, fleeing from Oklahoma City. We don't know who's driving until we stop them and we don't know why they're running unless we catch them. It's that simple.

What if McVeigh would have fled away at a high speed and a municipal officer, or county deputy, would have started the chase?

A supervisor fearful of being blamed for not stopping the chase, and bear in mind a supervisor will never, ever be second guessed by the administration for stopping it in fact the opposite is true. What if they would have told the officer to kill the pretty lights and sirens and return to their jurisdiction? Granted, most cases don't have the mass pain associated with such devastation that McVeigh caused, which resulted the massive joint gathering of so many law enforcement personnel to get the bad guy, but let's get back to the more common.

That could have been a local officer, with a department that so stringently chastises if you dare pursue and they let him just drive away. It could have happened so easily. If the next landmark, that was so callously detonated occurred the next day, and was at the hands of the bad guy we were ordered not to chase, who's really at fault here?

I remember when I got my first "new" police car. Kinda like a sixteen-year-old's first ride. It was back in 1994 and I'll tell you about that in a minute. I was so used to decade old police cars that I used to make it point to put the starting mileage, on the radio, at every opportunity. Not just the last couple of digits on the odometer but the whole thing, loud and clear, usually starting with "two-hundred thousand" and on and on. Wrong ear heard me do that one night and that was that. It was an embarrassment for our citizens in scanner land to hear the truth, at that time.

Allow me to tell you a couple of more memorable pursuits I've been in.

Probably the most memorable was one involving our new police chief and my "good old" Plymouth. After years of abuse (not at my hands) this car had a top speed of about seventy miles per hour, downhill, with a back wind and ice covered streets. This particular period had my rusting black and white with numerous problems, including an on-going fuel filter problem, brought on partially by years of about 13-octane fuel (I think we got the stuff that they could filter from the bottoms of old storage tanks). If I got to a speed of about forty, maybe forty-five, it would choke and the accelerator was useless until I got down to about twenty-five an hour and then I'd try to pick up steam again.

This night the new chief was spending time with each officer, in the field and I was destined to catch a drunk driver and show her my skills. Well, we see a newer model Mustang, at an intersection a couple of blocks away, doing power turns and doughnuts.

I start after the car, radio our dispatch and field troops about the incident and, as we head south, my cruiser starts its usual battle between thick gas and choking for air. As I get to forty it slows to twenty and on and on. Really frustrating, especially I imagine, for a new chief that has the highest of expectations and sees first hand the equipment her officers have to contend with. Well, I try to maintain visual while the other cars close in. Several roadblocks and numerous old police cars later we terminate the chase when we lose sight of the suspect.

He, in his 5.0 liter sportster, along with a passenger that has little control of his future at the moment, pass the last intersection at over one-hundred miles an hour. So they got away, you say? Nope, this ended like many do.

The suspect continued south, turned out the lights and, unknown to him, the road ends. A few minutes later a call comes in of a loud crash about three miles from where this all started. The driver knew he was in trouble when the asphalt turned to gravel and the gravel ended at the base of a tree.

We find the crash and locate both the driver, who was uninjured and drunk, and the passenger, who was lying in a field by the passenger door. His leg was shattered and I believe he either lost the leg or it was now useless for the rest of his life, which was by the way, in his late teens.

The tree they hit, as investigation later confirmed, had an area about six feet off the ground where the front bumper hit it. Airborne, lose a leg, change your life forever and all brought on by beer muscles, a lack of care for others and a sick attempt to get out of a traffic ticket, for that's all he would have received. One traffic ticket.

Another memorable chase involved a hot rod in every sense of the word. A hole in the hood displayed a tower of engine parts, all gleaming of chrome and an exhaust that dared any to wait patiently at its side at a traffic light. Well, as we pass, I see a taillight that's burned out and a signal light that's stuck on. That was the extent of the violation(s) and I turned around on the vehicle just to advise the driver of the defect. I didn't even plan on writing him a ticket, just a friendly notification of a burned out bulb. Well, he sees me turn around (no other cars on the road), the carb opens up, the tires wail and the chase is on.

Now, and I said I'd tell you about my first new police car, here it is. I had a new Caprice, with a very hot engine and I'd been in it for three days. Bear in mind, I waited forever for a good police car and I'm one chase away, if it ends badly, in going back to a Studebaker.

Well, we head north on an old highway and I'm running about ninety miles an hour, right on his heels and maybe using about a half pedal. He's mine, regardless. Well, he picked the wrong car to run from, the wrong time of day (no traffic) and his five thousand-dollar engine must have had the flu. One puff of smoke, car fluids cover the road and he slows to stop and, like always, now he wants to play nice. Too bad, so sad.

He gets to stare at that wrong end of my gun sights and tell me what a God-fearing, mother-loving, good Christian boy he is. Turned out though, as the years passed and he was forced to grow up, he was a good man. Still needs to grow up a bit, but at least this chase ended with him having the chance to grow up.

One final chase I've got to pass on then we'll run in another direction. I was backing "the Sarge" on a traffic stop and the driver (no passengers) had a suspended driver's license, which means in our city, he's going to jail. Well, Sarge tells him to step out, he asks why and Sarge, not a huge fan on the public relations aspect of life at that time says your license is suspended and you're going to jail.

The driver pauses, says, "It's not gonna happen," the dirt flies and off we go. I handle the radio traffic, freeing the primary chase car to keep up and be as safe as possible and we wind up on the outskirts of a neighboring town, about fifteen miles from our turf.

One big problem, when a chase gets out of the city, is that we're usually lost. Bad guy usually has an idea where he's headed but we use landmarks to direct assisting officers. Many times the directions, in the heat of a chase, are to turn left at a big tree, by the blue car, past the roadkill, you get the idea. Anyway, he makes it to a deserted driveway, at a farmhouse and his garage door is raising as the Sarge moves in.

Now, this is a real bad scenario. The driver knows where he is, whose home, where the guns are, etc. Sarge runs to the garage, holds the now closing garage door open with his shoulder, since one hand has a gun trained at the garage door and a flashlight in the other. Turns out an older house has an older garage door and it doesn't pop open when met with resistance.

I fly up, hear the Sarge's shoulder cracking and, after clearing the garage as best as possible, I hit the garage door opener (next to the door the bad guy just entered). Turns out there were two garage doors, with two separate openers and, you guessed it, the door next to my supervisor, who's on the receiving end of a spinal adjustment, tells me in no uncertain terms that patrolman Vanna picked the wrong button.

Imagine the thought of the guy that ran from us busting out of the door, at any time, with guns in hand, while I'm wiping the tears from my eyes from one of those deep down belly laughs. Strangely, Sarge didn't share my humor at the time.

Let's look at common sense, legal aspects of pursuits that line the pockets of so many attorneys. No one, even the most hardened, veteran cop, wants to respond to a bad crash, much less see it in front of him (her) or certainly to be a part of it. The true pain and gruesome finality of broken, bleeding, lifeless bodies is often a tragic result of a high-speed chase.

I can think of nothing, nothing that better exemplifies the "damned if you do, damned if you don't" reality of car chases. Every television set in America has portrayed the end result of chases that go bad, usually with the innocent being involved in the aftermath. Where do you draw the line, if one has to be drawn, that still allows us to do our jobs?

One very important step, and the State of Oklahoma has recently in the past few years implemented in its basic police academies, is high speed and defensive tactics in operating a police car. Specialized instructors test the recruits' abilities, under very stringent conditions and you must show your aptitude and ability or you don't graduate. If we train our officers to drive safely, under the worst of conditions, then we must support them in doing their job in the field, and that means allowing them to chase the bad guy.

That brings up a sensitive area with me that I could only pray the defense attorneys and juries would agree with. Why is it we, the police, that are always portrayed as the instigators of the problem by chasing, immediately laying blame directly at our feet, and not the fact "they" are the ones that started all this by running?

We, the police, do not want to drive through your neighborhoods, which by the way is where our kids play too, at mach speeds. At least we do watch out for kids, family pets, name it, while the true person to blame could care less about the harm "they" are so callously opening the door to.

A few years back, the courts made running a roadblock a felony. Now, and we've been trying for years, our lawmakers will again vote on making it a felony (that means potential, though not realistic, prison time) if you try to elude a "pursuing" officer. The obvious problem, though, is that wrecks will still happen, the innocent will still be killed and the lawsuits will continue to be filed at a maddening rate.

Fine, fill the courtrooms with briefs and sue for as long as their bank account keeps you interested, but, sue the one that runs and not the police for trying to do their job.

One solution, though about as likely as seeing Elvis and Jimmy Hoffa playing checkers, is to afford the police "qualified immunity" from the results of pursuits, but and I'll give you this, if they performed in the manner consistent with their training. If an officer commits a "willful" act of negligence, which means to act without "due regard" to life, that's one thing. If, during a chase, the officer can pick up some ground on a bad guy by cutting through your back yard, taking out your fence that protects your kids while they play in the sandbox, then of course they brought it on themselves. But, if the "bad guy" takes out that same fence, and drags your sandbox (or kids) as he flees, don't blame the officer because he was following with his siren wailing.

Our goal is to stop pain, not create it, but please lay the blame for the pain where it truly belongs. Do we want our police so limited, so afraid to do their jobs, that we wind up with a force of once dedicated public servants now afraid to enforce the law?

Where do we, as citizens that really have the input to effect the decisions of our nation's lawmakers, draw the line? If a suspect runs from us, on foot, and runs in front of a car, or truck, or train, whatever, and he/she gets hurt or killed, is that the fault of the police as well? I'll bet you wouldn't have to look far to find a $1,200 suit that would think so.

This issue will only continue to deteriorate if we don't address it, now. Folks, we're laying the groundwork to not only expect but, by our lack of actions and support, encourage an offender to flee. If the penalties for running from the law remain lenient, and the blame for the suffering is guided by the "deep pockets" theory, (suing the ones with the money—cities rather than the criminals), then when will this madness end?

To conclude, I've been a productive officer, with countless arrests and thousands of tickets and I've never, ever been sued, not once. (Excuse me while I find some genuine imitation wood to knock on.) I say this not to brag but to drive home a point, so please don't think my words are based on past events or bitterness that a $1,200 suit got the best of me. I have seen great cops, on the receiving end of wrongful lawsuits and it really is sickening.

They are never the same afterwards because, from what I've seen, the city/town that employs them has washed their hands of the whole thing and yet another once productive cop has felt the true feeling of being on your own. All for caring so much that they put on a uniform and wanted nothing more than to protect your families and "catch" the bad guys.

Hope they don't run!

CHAPTER NINE
Out On Patrol

To date, the closest I've come to being shot in the line of duty was back in my reserve days. A couple of us headed to a remote area where somebody, who knew somebody, who talked to somebody, on and on, said a dope field was growing.

We walked forever, in tremendous heat and we actually stumbled within about a quarter mile of the field, which was being tended. A few shots rang out over our heads, they whistled through the brush and trees around us and then it ended just as soon as it had begun.

In those days we didn't have fancy utility uniforms or clearly marked raid jerseys. We put on a shirt, jeans, tick repellent and away we went. Anyway, the shots were a warning, from one group protecting its field from rivals and, when they were eventually caught, "they" were "crow hunting" and knew nothing of the dope field.

The judge who heard the case of our "crow hunters" and the unfortunate place they chose to hunt felt, at the preliminary hearing, that they weren't tied sufficiently to the crime of cultivating marijuana.

By the way, the 600+ plants that we pulled up had just been watered and the five-gallon buckets in the possession of our "crow hunters" were for, what else, holding the crows (funny, I've never seen crow on a menu or even the most outback of kitchen tables). No doubt they didn't want to disturb the ecosystem. Gee, what nice guys.

A dozen things should go through a cop's mind when he/she decides to start patrolling. Traffic enforcement sounds simple but, the longer you're a cop and the more cars you stop, the more careless you become. That's the last thing a street cop likes to admit to. I'd love to say I've never fit in that category but I have, many times.

Don't be so quick to judge. You do the same thing, a couple of thousand times and tell me you don't expect the same ending. Sure, we're all careful the first time we make contact (hopefully) with a traffic offender, but, after a few years on the street our guard immediately drops when we hear few "yes sir, no sir's" or the driver is a "no threat" female.

It has been proven, by the coldest of cop killers, that if you flatter a cop's ego you lower their shields. Remember when I told you that teen "criminals" will appeal to their parents sense of obligation, so will a "bad guy" appeal to a cop's expectation of respect for the uniform.

Let me give you the ultimate let down for a cop that lives to catch drunk drivers. We see many, obvious traffic violations, usually weaving all over the road. You plant the spotlight to burn a hole in the back of the suspected offenders head and see one of two clues that tell you what you've seen many times before. Either an old felt hat (usually brown) or bluish-purple hair, barley visible over the dashboard, with the steering wheel resembling a halo. It's one of our cherished elderly and they're either lost or driving at night and the lights certainly distract their attention.

I've got one story I've got to pass on. A fellow officer I greatly respect, Mike Denton, a lowly patrolman at the time (but still a gentleman) and now a corporal, stopped a car that he suspected to be an intoxicated driver. All over the road, making turns where there weren't curves, you get the idea.

Well, I was a backing officer and we quickly found a brown felt hat and uniquely tinted hair. They were almost two centuries old between them and they epitomized why we harbor respect for our elders.

Though now over two-hundred miles from home, the trip started as a short jaunt to the outskirts of town. They got disoriented, fueled several times and kept getting farther from where they planned on being many hours before.

Initially, Mike stopped the car, found both to be sober and told them to drive carefully, after being told they were fine and help was not necessary. It was a few more violations, while directly behind them and after just letting them go, that he knew help was necessary.

We were two blocks from a motel and without any thought process, the skinny wallet cops are used to, jumped at the chance. Actually, it was the wallet of a dispatcher (Mark Harper, and he's done it all in the name serving the public) that a credit card secured the room and we all pitched in.

When we briefed the shift of the story that's about to follow, every cop and dispatcher took a few bills, that they could ill well afford, to help the cause. That, my friends, is the source from which law enforcement blood flows.

To continue, we secure the room (the only one left, believe it or not, kinda no room at the inn stuff!) and we have the hotel clerk notify us when they rise for the day. Well, I get off at 7am and head to the hotel, with Mike ready to join me but an agenda full of things that have to get done lead him elsewhere. I go to the lobby, visit with the clerk and await the arrival of our special guests.

The gentleman, a spry octogenarian plus ten, is bent at the waist, every day of his life. We all have crutches but his cane, though not a setback, is as common a tool as a hand is to a racquetball player. I offer breakfast but he politely says he doesn't have the means (money) and, when I inform him it's part of the room and charity is no longer an issue, he digs in symbolic of the last supper, and she holds her own as well.

I eventually determine that the initial trip, to deliver brownies to a church member, should have been about fifteen miles, round trip. They had driven over two-hundred miles and were too proud to ask for help. I guess if, like them, I'd been on this planet for about two centuries between them I'd feel pretty knowledgeable in the ways of life myself.

Anyway, we needed help and we knew just where to turn, our chaplain on-call. Turns out it was Reverend Pirtle's time in the chute and he was there almost before I hung up the phone. Not only did he arrange lunch, and gas for the car but he determined the nearest relative, the son of the gentleman, resided in a neighboring state and all who knew these senior angels had scouts on their path.

I must point out, though I wish I'd have asked his name, a traveler and his family saw me greet our weary travelers, figured out the basics of the scenario and put a twenty dollar bill in my hand before I could turn him down. Just so you know, it went into the older gentleman's pocket, but not before it was deposited into my heart. Thanks. You got the makings of a great cop!

Well, we finally track down the family, they load up a van full of worried relatives and the good reverend escorts them to the chow line while I take their cruiser to the nearest gas station. It was amazing, and at first I hoped the gas gauge was broken for it didn't even move, but, they were about out. Fumes had gotten me to the gas pumps but would surely have left our dearest guests on the side of the road in below freezing temperatures, with only their pride to keep them warm.

It would have definitely ended badly. I've seen enough of that on the side of the road and I wouldn't trade this for anything in the world.

To make a long, and wonderful, story short, the family arrives, a group hug like you've never seen follows and, after a few kisses on the cheek and quick snapshots, off they go. It's not one of the stories you make movies about but our shift wouldn't have traded it for gold.

I've said it before and I'll say again. It's what we do; it's who we are. Please don't try to figure it out because you would have already tried to apply to one of our sister agencies if it came to you as thoughtlessly as taking our next breath does to us.

Of course incidents like that are the exception. Some stops turn out badly. If you know many veteran police officers all have had an experience that's right out of science fiction. You're behind a car and, for no reason known to mankind, the hair on your neck stands up and your body shivers.

Whom-ever is either behind the wheel or hiding in the darkness of the backseat has alerted a sense that tells you bad things are waiting for you. It doesn't happen often and even the best of the best will volunteer that they never stopped that car, despite what they do.

That used to really upset me, at first, until I thought of the street experience that they could claim and I was trying to establish. My initial thought was, "If whoever is in that car is that bad, then he's the one I want, the one I scour these streets for night after night." After I continued to grow up as a cop, I started to understand where they were coming from, but I still say I'd have stopped the car. Should I have?

I finally stepped back from my invincible cocoon and thought of all the police officers that have been shot to death on the simplest of traffic stops. I recall a story of an officer that was a cop for many years stopped many, many cars and always exited his car and walked to the driver's side door.

For a reason more powerful than we probably care to know (maybe the Good Lord?), he decided to walk on the passenger side and only one head was visible, and it was behind the steering wheel where it's supposed to be. Maybe the hair on the back of that "blue-collar" neck stood at attention.

Anyway, he approaches the trunk, to the back door and, as he looks at the driver (staring in his rear-view mirror), he a sees a man lying in the rear floorboard, with a .45 caliber pointed at the rear, driver's side window. Had he (she) taken the usual route he would be dead today. Another statistic.

If you get too paranoid you're of no use to the force and if you're too omnipotent you're of no use to yourself, much less your community. Don't forget you must humble Goliath by your presence and reinforce The Pope's faith in humanity by your actions.

Well, I said we we're going to stop a car so let's get with it. I have two decisions here, whether I "troll" for offenders or, if in a sneaky (or maybe a tired) mood, find a highly traveled and sparsely lit patch of prehistoric grass (asphalt).

I usually have two determining factors that determine whether I un-cloak and chase you or if I just "tap" my pretty colored lights and let you know I saw you. First, if what you did was flagrant, you made it easy for me and here I come, so hook up that seat belt that was probably lying unbuckled at your side. Second, if you peaked my curiosity, maybe it was the seeing five heads as we met and two as you passed. Or, and I love this one, you wave when you see me, immediately signal, but you're still on a straight road with nowhere to turn. Ding, ding, ding, hello. No E-ticket needed here.

For whatever reason, we have our target car in our sights and we start to hit the lights, first telling our dispatcher where we are, at least at the moment. I say at least because at any moment the muffler vomits black smoke and the chase is on.

For this stop, it's business as usual and we approach the driver, probably too carelessly. We give our hellos, tell them why we disrupted their day and ask for the expected.

I'll give you a hint. If you start the contact by reaching for your wallet, patting your pockets and utter that you must have left it at the house, we really are smarter than that. We now know it's either suspended or you don't want us to really know who you are. Either way, if we're good at what we do, you might as well come clean because everybody, especially cops, hate getting lied to and we get kaa-kaa from the very best, so we know where this is going.

I promise you, honesty now will make it a whole lot easier, and the possibility of leniency deteriorates with every pocket that recently, and usually fictitiously, once held your "right" to drive.

I'll give you a couple of tips that might, just might, help keep your driving record in good shape. First of all, if when we pass you see my brake lights and the start of a three point turn, if you're guilty, find a safe place to pull over and we'll be right with you.

Many times, if you weren't too excessive with the long pedal next to the brake, the simple act of voluntarily pulling over might tilt the balance in your favor.

Next, and usually the ultimate factor, is your driving record. One speeding ticket in ten years tells us you're either a careful driver or you've been very fortunate. On the other hand, if you've had a dozen tickets, for a myriad of offenses, in a relatively short period of time, then settle back and prepare for the request of your autograph to be forthcoming.

We give breaks to the deserving, not the B.S. artists. And whatever you do, don't be nice at the beginning only to develop an attitude when you see the ticket book. We will remember that your words were to fool us, and falsely flatter, in other words, lie. Most likely, we will see you again and one ticket can blossom into a handful, very quickly.

Got a great story that happened to a former campus cop, that I worked with briefly, who pursued a career as an Oklahoma State Trooper. Well, as law enforcement families do, he'd drop by to say hi to his old family and relay the stories he'd experienced. He told us that he was working the turnpikes (highways) and stopped an elderly gentleman for driving about 80mph, back when the speed limit was 55.

Upon stopping the gentleman he inquired why he was driving so fast and, without thinking, he took a hand-crafted piece of metal, about the size and shape of a ping pong paddle. He stated he saw a road sign that said "speed radar enforced" and, he calmly but with street-smart confidence says, that whenever he sees such a sign, he places the metal contraption over his pacemaker and holds it there, driving as fast as he safely can, until he gets back to a safe area to resume his travels.

Our new trooper was left with a blank look on his face, gave him an "A" for ingenuity and, so he wouldn't start laughing while on the side of the road, he sent him on his way with a stern warning.

By the way, the plausibility of such an interaction with our radars has since been investigated, so, don't even try it. It takes all kinds and truthfully, such contacts help keep our minds open to the human side of law enforcement.

Something else that must be passed on, just in the event you've been asleep for a while. The Interstate Compact, in as few words as possible, means that if you get a ticket in "Fredville, USA," and figure there's no need paying it since you'll never be back there, think again. If you don't pay the ticket, or at least contest it in court, your driving privileges will be suspended everywhere, and will stay that way until that ticket is paid for and until you're re-instated in whatever state issued you your license. It gets really costly, so, you might just think twice.

Also, while I'm on the topic, this is addressed to those that immediately start the tears from the second we approach (the guys as well). It used to be an unwritten rule, that if they cry and you *don't* issue a ticket, you can count on getting a complaint.

Don't ask me why, short of the possibility that, if you're that emotional over a minor infraction, your perception of our demeanor might not seem to be as professional as expected, even if we were. So, when the tears dry, they're replaced with anger, then they manifest what really happened to what they believed happened, or should have, and bingo, they complain.

Again, it's really easy to get complained on, even if you do the best job you possibly can, so be prepared. This is where your past credibility with your department's supervisors is so vital.

Believe it or not, we do make traffic stops at times, just to be nice. If you have one taillight burned out, but the other one works, then why don't we just leave you alone? I'll tell you. If one light goes out, that leaves just one. If the other goes out, how many are left? Now, with no light emitting from the rear of your car, does that not make it hard to see you at night?

Well, here comes the drunk driver or reckless driver. The reckless driver might not see you in time to stop and the drunk driver might not see you at all. If we could prevent even one wreck, just one, by "inconveniencing" you with a traffic stop, so be it. Besides, how many of you check your tail lights every time you start to drive? And if you're fast enough to push on your brakes and run around to see if those lights are operative, you don't need a car to get around.

To say an officer is simply on patrol is far from our actual intent. The methods of patrol vary from officer to officer and several unique ways still produce great results. The best that comes to mind is to be seen in an area, drive a few blocks, hide in the shadows and then return to the area you just circled.

Many burglars get an unconscious relief once we've passed and they go back to their evil ways. Often, you can drive right up on them before they realize you've returned.

Another is to saturate an area, if you're fortunate enough to have enough officers, usually three or four (for lucky towns), that can realistically saturate. You start with a loose perimeter, usually several blocks of businesses or one isolated neighborhood, if placing your emphasis on residential patrol. You start out wide and slowly move in, with the exception of one unit that moves in quickly.

The latter is utilized to flush our quarry and the rest of the pack tries to make contact before our prey has retreated back into the brush. You're lucky if it works once for every thousand tries, but, what fun it is when it does.

The least common, but by far the most fun, is to just drive up on something, with bad guys usually the farthest thing from your mind and you're probably thinking about food, or coffee, or court, or the fight you had before you left the house, name it. Anyway, you see a crime and it's all instinct from here. Even the coolest of veterans usually broadcast an octave higher and often get the most common of streets mixed up.

Forget using even the simplest of police codes, for plain talk usually erupts, often resembling a bad Mel Tillis impersonation. If it ends well, and that means the bad guy in jail, then take a minute and playback the audio recording from the Dictaphone.

You want a humbling experience, which is actually what we all need every now and then, then play it back, and not just in private, in front of the whole shift. Those giggles and one-liners will possibly bridge the gap that might have unknowingly been built, even more strengthening the bonds we hopefully all hold for each other.

If you're a supervisor, be adult enough to realize you are still human, a true street cop at heart and give your subordinates a chance to see you squirm a little. To truly be an effective supervisor they must respect the person inside those stripes, and that means the cop that was, still is and hopefully will always be a rookie at heart.

One of the more common, and potentially dangerous calls we receive, is the dreaded domestic disturbance. I'll not go into the details of the harm suffered by all with this nature of call, the worst being the kids that see what they have no control to resolve, but often they wrongfully take the blame, or at least try to "make all better."

Our department utilizes the services of one of our officers, Sonya DeArmond, to try to "make all better" from our side. She, in addition to all the duties every officer is responsible for, follows up on every single domestic situation that, regardless of the degree of severity, required our intervention.

Let me say a word about Sonya. If she ran for governor, I'd be honored to protect the grounds of the governor's mansion at night, just knowing someone of her caliber was sleeping inside. She's that good, and I'm a better person for having known, and worked, with her. Yes, she makes mistakes. Yes, I make mistakes. Yes, every umpire, ticket taker, appellate judge, investor, every profession makes mistakes. Learn from it, live with it and let's move on.

Anyway, back to what she does best. One wrong phone call, at the wrong time, and you could actually start a domestic, not salvage one. Instead of the blood and ugly, and there's plenty of that, let me tell you of a more memorable experience in this sensitive area.

We respond, as usual, to a domestic fight-in-progress and prepare for the worse. Well, a few years earlier, the laws reference to domestic disturbances was amended to include our securing any weapon that was involved, and maintain custody of the same for potential evidentiary value. That, I imagine, was intended to include guns, knives, baseball bats, tire irons, whatever.

So, we arrive at the scene, separate the involved parties (fortunately, no kids home this time) and the male, for a change, has suffered the brunt of the fight. His head is split from eye to ear and he's bleeding everywhere, with his "better half" not yet satisfied with the outcome.

We secure her in handcuffs and, given that she possesses no signs of physical trauma, even taking credit for being the victor of this battle (we've been here before and no doubt will return again) and she's placed under arrest for domestic assault and battery. True to the letter of the law, we then determine what weapon of mass destruction was used to inflict such damage to her beloved's skull.

It was, as investigation determined, a frozen Maine lobster. A three pound crustacean that, for the rest of its now thawing days, will be referred to a State's Exhibit #1.

I guess you had to be there.

I spoke early on about the time I was "shot at" while searching the plains for a marijuana field. I came extremely close to dying that day, but not just at the hands of those bad guys. Nor was it a lapse in officer safety training, it was my pride that almost did me in.

You know by now that I was just four pounds heavier than a large sack of produce when I first put on a uniform. In an attempt to "bulk up," which was before the days I could afford a bullet-proof vest, I would wear an extra sweatshirt or two, anything to enhance the skeletal physique I so hated, at least in the early days.

When the excitement was over, and the marijuana plants were pulled up by hand in the scorching heat, we start back to our vehicles. Due to the extra clothing, and with no water, I began to feel dizzy, then nauseous, then my captain saw my usually hyper pace slowing.

He calls me to stop and, immediately upon looking into my face, he sheds my clothing. I was ghost white, with no sweat left in my thin body and if I lose it out here, from heat stroke, miles from the nearest road and before the days of cellular phones or "extra" walkie-talkies, I was in real trouble.

Remember that if I wore extra clothing to be one of the guys, in their eyes, I surely wouldn't ask them to slow down or take a breather for my benefit. It was an embarrassment too, when they peel layer after layer of clothing, wondering what "Cookie Doctor" to send me to if/when they get me back to air-conditioning.

It takes several things to be a successful cop, especially ability and heart. Well, I bulked up with clothing so my fellow officers wouldn't doubt my ability and I covered my heart with so many layers of clothing that it could have cost me my life. Rather an ironic way to have gone.

Remember, you're not a cop out of size, or color, or any other obvious outside characteristic. You're a cop from what's inside and I had both ability and heart, but it would be years before I would prove it to myself.

CHAPTER TEN
Driving A Desk

You might wonder how a cop could ever forget, while still wearing a uniform, how to be a cop. It's a simple word, but, so devastating when the expected amnesia sets in.

The word, simply, is "desk," and when the sole purpose of your ass is to polish a chair and your eyes are needed only to gaze upon reports, you're well on your way. As a rule, you've either done very well, or you're in trouble, if your field of honor is a desktop.

The higher you climb up the ladder of success, the less time you'll spend doing what you've yearned to do all your life. You are rewarded for your accomplishments by being promoted, and yet you're removed from where you fought to be, the place from where-in you made all those accomplishments.

I'll start at the lower echelon of administration, usually a lieutenant for smaller departments and a captain for the larger forces. At this level, your patrol car merely takes you to and from the office and unless a command decision is needed in the field, that's where you'll spend your day. And I stress day here, for your contact with the nightlife is usually limited to reading what they've done.

It becomes common place to field complaints and the longer you hear the complaints and spend your nights at home watching TV, the greater distance you place between understanding what the field troops did, and why.

If I was a police chief, and I already had in "my twenty" so I could be free to be a chief, I'd have my administrative personnel spend at least a little time in the field. The scenery might just do them some good, though most likely, dependent on how long they've driven a rolltop, they'd probably just be in the way.

It's a necessary evil that so much paperwork is associated with the law enforcement profession. Each piece of paper, regardless of how trivial at the time, can grow to enormous levels of importance if not submitted in perfect form, and that means ultimately approved by a member of the administration.

Well, the chief, assistant chief, and the like are far too busy with politics and public relations so, the job is yours. And, of course, when the lawsuits grace your desk, after the trickle-down theory has run its gauntlet, your name is surely included on the list. Remember, the lawyers know where the money is and now that your check is just big enough to contemplate a much needed vacation or addition to your home, the $1,200 suits add your name to the *golden* list.

Granted, it's the city they're after but must they incriminate your actions before they can discredit the chief's office, and finally, the city's coffers are within reach. Either way, once the thought of a lawsuit is born, it's the legal profession that wins, regardless of whose victorious in a courtroom, for a bill is forthcoming, regardless.

A solution to this madness? You bet, I got one. In the event we are sued, and the decision is in our favor, let's make it routine for the attorney, law firm, whatever that first brought this suit to reimburse the effected officers, supervisors, administrators and finally the city, for all costs encumbered.

That means every fee, every hour of overtime, every dollar we lost for not being able to work our necessary part-time jobs, child care, emotional suffering, discredit to our reputation, name it.

The ball started rolling by forcing the bearer of "frivolous" lawsuits to compensate accordingly, so let's take it one step farther. If a true injustice was done, so be it. If you want something for nothing, at least in the eyes of the courts, then go for it, knowing full well you'll pay if you lose. I'll bet that'll clean off a few dockets.

Along the same tone, though slightly off track, is the need for the veteran officers to remember their basic police skills, and that means either remedial training, and you'll have union contracts to contend with, or a return to the night shift. Unfortunately, with seniority is an expectation, or even a right, to work what shift you want.

The older you are, the more common that means day shift only, with weekends off. Now don't think for a moment that seniority shouldn't have its rewards, and I've seen it too many times, they get to where they couldn't safely function on a shift other than the same one, month after month, year after year.

In a way, it's almost a sick way to groom an officer for desk duty. We almost support their losing contact with what the other shifts are doing and, when promoted to lower administrative duties, it's no wonder they've lost the feel for the drunk catchers and the night prowlers. So, do what then? Protect them and others by placing them behind a desk? All driven by the guise that it's for a job well done?

Let me stop here to stress the importance of veteran officers, senior officers if you will, and what a vital role they "can" play in really solidifying a department. Especially in a smaller department for all the rookies' eyes are trained on their actions. If they have lost the insight on being a rookie, then crawl out from behind that desk and set them straight. Use tact, for they do deserve our respect, but recognize a need for a friendly push "back" in time.

If you have just inherited a desk, prepare for criticism. Every action you take will be met with either jealousy or apathy. It's a common theme that really shines in law enforcement, specifically, those that can, do, those that can't tell you how to, usually from behind a desk or in a classroom. Regardless, you're not on the streets so you already have to justify why you're good enough to command their respect and attention.

In my humble opinion, there's only one way to steer a desk and still garnish the respect of the field troops. Be a field trooper, at least at heart, and that may mean making decisions that won't be popular in your bosses' eyes.

You are now in a catch-22 position. If a given problem started at the top it falls to you and if it started at the bottom, it rises up to you. We could relate it to the life of a bakery chef. Either your cake will fall if you're too loud and careless or your biscuits will rise too far if not taken out of the heat, in time and handled with gloves. In either circumstance, can you see "getting burned" as an option if you act without due regard.

Sorry, I'll try to fall back down to earth. See? I lost track within the pages of a book. It's that easy.

Let's look at the other reason you're riding the wooden conference cruiser. You've stepped on it, or least somebody with stroke thinks so. How many times have we all heard the media say something like this, "The officer is currently assigned to desk duty pending a departmental investigation"?

Well, and you all know where I'm going with this, we've placed a direct correlation between doing wrong and riding a desk and though the desk is as vital of a role as a field officer, in a limited capacity, it will always be a necessary evil.

That's but one more reason that such a vast difference between blue-collar and white-collar employees exists, and always will. Never forget the blue-collar golden rule, "The more you physically do, the less you financially receive."

It's a good thing we don't don a badge for money or we'd never get anything done, we'd be too busy judging others. Lord knows your physical ability is certainly limited if you're imprisoned behind the contour of a high-back chair.

Do me a favor. All of those in administrative, secondary administrative, CEO's, presidents, vice presidents, lieutenants captain's, captain's of industry, etc, either go to your office first and read this paragraph or at least sit back and imagine staring at your desktop.

Now, slowly swivel your chair around and gaze at the walls and what do you see? Look hard at the plaques, awards, photographs and the like. Now, realistically, how many did you earn either prior to desk duty, or, did you receive just because of your desk duty, your official title?

If you earned them in the field, think of what you did to deserve them. If you earned an award, or even an honorary degree, since you've ridden a desk, was that for your actions behind a desk, or what led you to that desk, or just maybe, for the actions of the troops you command/supervise?

Give credit where it's due. If to yourself, great, but, if your troops brought you here, maybe you should lower that pride enough to remember how envious you were when those, undeservingly, took credit for the work of others, maybe even your work back as a recruit. Have you started to lose touch? I'm sure you're not alone.

And by the way, my previous offer still stands for you CEO's and captains of industry to spend a weekend mind-melding with us flat-foots. That's the second time I've challenged you, and I bet before I'm done (which hopefully will coincide with when you're done) you'll be challenged again. I'll even pay for it, if, hamburgers can substitute for milk fed veal and the linen napkins will resemble your tee shirt. No, I'm not that sloppy, in fact quite the opposite, but you definitely won't have a toilet attendant selecting your cologne.

I'll again stress that, despite the "bite" of several paragraphs, or even chapters, I'm not downing professionals merely because they're not a cop or because they do sit behind a desk all "day" long in business suits, or even if they're a lawyer. I respect the man, or woman, for the job they do, for the desire they have to be the very best and to take the credit, as well as the blame, for their actions. That includes cops, behind desks, if they're still cops at heart.

Let me tell you a common scenario that places such a vast canyon between the field troops and those superior officers that have an office. You, the office dweller, often begin a statement to us with a question, a question that we answer for you, and you're the boss here, the one that earned you an office by virtue of you're outstanding work in the field.

I wish I had a dollar (sorry, suits, that is an expression) for every time a supervisor that approves my work asks for details on the law. It became so frequent, even simple legal questions, that I initially lost respect for them, which means I would lose respect (unintentionally) for the many years of service they have provided to so many.

I now realize, due to the system, that we set up our newest office dwellers to fail, at least in the eyes of the field troops they now supervise, and yet they begin their new assignment with the desire to hopefully motivate and offer support. It is vital, in my opinion, that desk duty includes at least a minimum amount of continuing field service, coupled with on-going training side-by-side with the troops they command. This contact will benefit all by not only reminding the upper level supervisor's of where they came from, but where the future office dwellers will someday go.

We've looked briefly at the negative side of a desk, but and I always look for the rainbow, there are some positive aspects of mounting the mahogany that are very important. By the mere action of walking into an office, you have all but the most hardened at their most vulnerable.

This is an opportunity to either show support, and respect, or to lay the groundwork for starting the bridge between what we both have to do. That bridge can be either be a fallen log that covers a spring or the Golden Gate, it's up to you. And that goes for both the law enforcement world as well as the corporate way of life, for both afford the same stress factors when a subordinate passes through the wooden door frame that unintentionally separates us all.

I can think of nothing that motivated me more, regardless of what my occupation was at the time, than the supportive words of an employer. A pat on the back can yield immediate and long term results, if said with sincerity, as can negative feedback yield a disastrous outcome if spouted without first thinking.

Remember, when any of us walk into the office of an employer, and don't forget your sensitive areas are protected by a desk and ours are exposed (you know what I mean), every word is taken as gospel. Please don't blame the motivation of your troops if your words drove morale into the ground.

Most importantly, we will never, ever forget what words pass your lips. It's also a given that those words, once we get leave your office, will fill the ears of every cop (and civilian co-worker) that either saw us go into your office or that we see for many shifts to come.

Subordinates listen to their own and word will spread to every troop well before you close your desk drawer, lock your office door and start a very cold engine on a police car that's been parked for quite a while. Ironically, that police car you drive is far superior to the fleet vehicles that the night cops will have at their access, and they need cars to catch the bad guys, not to get to and from work.

There's one other group of folks that sit behind a desk that commands our utmost respect, and though that could include the experts in the communications field, I'm referring to those with physical disabilities that restrict "field" operations. Maybe you're a cop that got injured in the line of duty, or you've lived your life in a wheelchair.

Your jurisdiction is a desktop and I have no doubt you could teach us all a thing or two about how to truly earn a living. I thank you all and if I may ask a favor, would you talk to those that just "earned" a desk and tell them what's coming, what to expect and what we really need from you.

To jump back to the happy side of enforcement, I'll never forget this. We respond to an automobile accident, but this one involves a truck that went from the street into the den of a house, situated at an intersection.

Fortunately, and we habitually expect the worse, we find no death or serious injury. We do, however, find a rather large gentleman pinned between a front bumper, a beautiful desk and what used to be an upright wall.

Feeling no pain (thanks to a brewery or vineyard) and obviously quite embarrassed, given the uninvited attention and that he was dressed *very* casual, stated quite simply, "I've never felt this much pressure sitting behind a desk."

That kind of says it all. You realize it's an important and necessary job, but you unknowingly expect a certain amount of protection when your toes push your chair into that petrified area, beneath the drawer, the one that, without words, expectedly protects you when, and where, you're most vulnerable.

CHAPTER ELEVEN
You Get Promoted

Dependent on the size of the respective agency you work for, getting promoted is either the acknowledgment that you've done a good job or you've painted the chief's house. Co-workers that respect you will congratulate and those that don't will still congratulate you, but if you could be a fly on the wall when they talk about promotions, what a different story you'd hear.

We all fight to achieve those stripes, bar(s)/clusters and even eagles and shortly thereafter, we wonder why in the hell we even put in for it. Sure, everybody wants to succeed, to know that you've done a good job and certainly for the pride your family will achieve from your accomplishments if, of course, you still have a family to come home to.

It's truly amazing how such simple acts of enforcement now take on a whole new meaning. How we used to live for a pursuit, and now that it's your decision to stop it or allow it and everything that follows is at your discretion, it's time to build your first supervisory ulcer.

Actually, your promotion comes with a raise, not for the title, but for the added medical expenses. Antacids will be as common a nutritional aid as water is to a plant.

We've all seen adequate street cops who were wonderful supervisors, and likewise, we've seen rotten supervisors that were dynamic street cops. What is this magical transformation that so quickly can turn our wonderful careers inside out?

If I could sum it all up I'd use two words. *Responsibility and Power.* With one comes the other yet, prior to promotion, we had no difficulty at all with either. Every job we've all ever held had a certain degree of power and all were recognized to maintain an obvious degree of responsibility. The big difference is that, prior to promotion, our responsibilities were usually isolated to one or two specific tasks and responsibility stopped at our actions, not the actions of others.

Now, we have the power, by virtue of our promotion, to directly effect how our subordinates perform their given duties. Compound that with the responsibility that those actions were done correctly, and timely, and professionally, and respectfully, and with your knowledge, at all times and you get the idea.

It's amazing how many things we used to take for granted, as a patrolman, that now take on a whole new meaning. It's, hopefully, a re-birth of values that, just like the veteran officers we spoke of earlier that need to remember where they came from, that re-birth is now mandated by our new title.

An example, how about our appearance? The dry cleaners take care of the uniform, but what about all the pretties that we attach to it. Where they were shiny before, they must gleam now. And our boots, where they were dust free before, now they must appear as if they have never been on a pair of feet.

Why? Well, one of our new tasks is to ensure those under your umbrella of responsibility are up to standards and how can you, realistically, discipline if you yourself don't measure up.

Oh, it can, and has been done, but you'll immediately lose your troop's respect and if you can't handle the pressure, take an old uniform out of the closet and let someone else play boss. That's meant in no way to say that you don't deserve your new title, merely to stress that it's a whole new game, and your rules just got a whole lot more stringent.

If there was one thing that I would like to see as a requirement for new supervisors, it would be a collegiate course in humility. To respect the rank is a given, for many safe-guards, called policies, require respect, at least on the surface, for all those entrusted to supervisory status.

Remember the often used scripture that to the effect states it's easier for a camel to pass through the eye of a needle than for a rich man to enter the gates of heaven. In my opinion, it's not that money holds you back from the Pearly Gates, it's the way you now live your life since acquiring wealth.

Short of those that inherited their portfolios, most work many, many years to obtain their possessions and when you acquire things one stick of furniture at a time, it's hard to really realize exactly all that you own. With the more you get, the more you take for granted and along the same lines, the more you change, though it happens so slowly, literally years in the making, you don't realize it's happening.

Now, let's customize that to being promoted. You've worked many, many years to obtain a career to be proud of and, slowly but eventually, you amass a fortune that places you in the company of a select few.

Instead of stocks to adorn a safety deposit box you now affix stripes or shiny rectangular bars to adorn a uniform. You're now rich in the eyes of a patrolman, for achieving what you have, symbolic of a mail clerk that eventually made it to an upstairs, corner office (complete with a great, big, pretty desk). You've earned a right to both, but you're starting all over. You're a rookie again in many respects. Maybe if we remember that "humbling" time of our lives, our new transition will be one to be proud of, and, especially by those "downstairs."

My wish would be, for every supervisor or supervisor to be, that we can extend the knowledge of experience into our new status yet maintain the yearning to learn that is inherent in every recruit.

Allow me to use an analogy that might fit better than I first thought. I initially became an officer to help, to serve, to chase and catch, all these things. I first started writing a book so that I could tell those that wonder, or wish to be, what to expect if you strap on a gun (legally).

At first I couldn't type enough, and dependent on the night that followed, I couldn't at times force myself in the direction of a keyboard. But when I did start typing again, it all came so crystal clear that I couldn't stop.

Well, that's how it is. You love dearly what you do and wouldn't trade it for all the hair your pets leave on the pillows, but you do get frustrated. As soon as the uniform is back on, it all comes back to you.

Just like when Miss Meow (our cat is Miss Mir) or Mr. Bark get out of the bath, curl up in your lap and yearn for every scratch behind the ears, you wouldn't trade their need for your contact for anything, that is what they live for. Their entire life means nothing more to them than each caress, symbolic of how we, as police officers, yearn to please our communities.

I know that's pushing literary nausea to the brink, but hang on. Compound that with the responsibility that you, the supervisor, now hold the mental scratching posts and foot long chew-bones that every pet is fed and, here we go, that every rookie can go home at the end of a shift to feed them, then you realize how deep this really goes. You're right, a Pulitzer Prize is definitely not forth coming.

I promise you all one thing, which is, that every person in the world has thought, in regards to their boss, that they could do a far better job than he/she has done. They tell you what to do, yet, no doubt in your mind you could do it much more efficiently, and caring, on and on.

When the day finally comes that you get to fill their shoes you unexpectedly earn a little more respect for their, now your, new position. This part of your career is not where the need for humility comes in, because, just as a rookie becomes a veteran, a new supervisor slowly lets the eye of the needle get a little bit smaller, day by day, if we lose sight.

A suggestion. Just like I put my wife's wedding band on my finger to keep me aware of my personal direction, the new supervisor should have a framed picture staring him/her in their eyes. It won't hold the image of our spouse, or our kids, or even our folks or the VIP that shook your hand when you got an award. It should bear a picture of you, in uniform, at your graduation from the police academy (or advancement from the mail room). When you might otherwise get a little too big for your uniform trousers, or $1,200 suit, such a reminder just might make your days as a supervisor, not to mention the lives of those under your tutelage, a very pleasant and beneficial experience.

After all, when we've all retired and have nothing left but memories, wouldn't pride in your knowledge, experience and compassion be a far more comforting flashback than the turbulence that you brought on, yet your pride forced you to blame others? Just another morsel for you to chew on.

We are, however, forced to be realistic. There will always be promotions were it's not warranted (brown nosers or politics, I've been accused of both) and those worthy of promotion, though respected for the job they do, will be unjustly patted on their back and sent away, allowing the before mentioned to succeed.

I would love for those that denied the truly worthy of promotion to look in the eyes of the deserving's children and explain why

Daddy or Mommy aren't where they deserve to be. Very few have the ethics to explain why, for they're the same group that don't have the guts to join us flatfoots for a weekend eye-opener.

For the supervisors of the future, if you want to succeed and be respected, follow this tip, and not only is it easy, it's vital. Ask those that you supervise for their opinion. As I said earlier, the *Wizard of Oz* did not bestow you with brains because the chief or sheriff bestowed you with stripes, bars, clusters or an office.

If you're confidant enough in your ability to lead, I pray you have the confidence to realize you don't know everything. Not only will asking for input make you a part of the team, and make them know that they are, but you might just learn something and I promise that you'll be well on your way to a promising career.

Remember this above all. You're actions will not only develop the supervisors of tomorrow, but hopefully keep them healthy (physically and mentally) to someday fill your shoes. You couldn't be more involved in the lives of the future than to be in the delivery room, clutching the pain stricken hand of the one you'll constantly take for granted, if you're not careful, and hopefully much smarter than I was.

CHAPTER TWELVE
A Cop's Day Off

If ever there was a play on words, a cop having a true day off goes over about as well as a condom in a collection plate. Rarely is there a day off not involving court, training, meetings and most likely, a part time job or two.

On those vary rare days that one of the above is not a factor, your neglected family wants, and needs, your undivided attention. The problem, you might ask, is that you, after all you do, need your undivided attention to selfishly recharge your mental batteries. If you do not allow yourself some quiet time, and that means to neglect your already neglected family, then you're no fun to be around even when given an opportunity to put employment and financial matters aside.

The solution? You tell me, put it in writing and I'll be happy to buy that book, but you must have walked in our shoes before your advice will be worthy of reading.

Despite doing this for about seventeen years, which means all of my daughter's life, the severity of it all never really hit home until recently. My daughter wanted something (there's a shock) and she spouted, without thinking, "If it's the day after you finished working you have to sleep all day, and, if it's the day before you go back to work, you have to go to sleep so you're not tired all night." Folks, that's a given without the courtroom, training, teaching, instructing, speaking, volunteering, on and on.

Probably the single leading incident that results in an argument at the Driver household is, when I am off, so many things are expected of me, and none are unrealistic. Most usually involve traveling a few miles to eat, or shop (for spuds that is, clothes are a definite "don't go there") or maybe a movie. That sounds fairly harmless, but, the last thing a cop, especially a veteran cop, cares to do on a day off is to be around people. Yet another irony in the law enforcement world. We can't wait for the opportunity to serve the public while on patrol yet we can't find a cave deep and dark enough to burrow in while we're not.

Everybody has heard the saying that a cop really hates to be in a crowd. The reason, simply enough, and a major obstacle that separates the white collar world from the cop world, is that we never get a chance to leave the office. Once you, the suits, turn off your computer, say goodnight to the secretary and start your leather upholstered ride, you're off work, off-duty to a degree. Sure, you may get a phone call at the house, or even have some work at home waiting on you, but you take a trip to the mall.

Just last night, I offered (to my dear wife's surprise) to go to the nearest big city for dinner. She jumped on the idea by agreeing after I said, "Do you want to?" Well, we had a nice dinner at one of my daughter's favorite spots and my wife said the words that curdle the toes of every male. Not just cops, and here we're all one (even the lawyers), she said, "Can I just drop in here (the mall) for a second? I know just what I want and just where it is."

To avoid the fight that's going to happen anyway I don't offer the usual resistance, knowing it's futile, symbolic of the drunk that I stop that pleads for the opportunity to just be followed home.

Well, we arrive at the mall and now I'm back at work. I glance at every male that has a pierced nose and look for a bulge in his shirt and not once have I not spotted at least one person that I've arrested before. The public is on the prowl for clothes, nick-knacks or Beanie Babies and I'm staring at every face, every mannerism, anything that could represent the criminal aspect.

My wife says it's paranoia, I say it's good common sense. Is it paranoia for a cop to instinctively sit with his back to the wall? Is it paranoia for a lawyer to see a cop behind him in the fast lane and not think he or she is about to get stopped just because they have a law degree. Enough, you get the idea and I'm straying from that rare day off.

A huge problem, that might not be thought of, is when, or if, to sleep. For those few veteran cops that don't use seniority as a "cop out" to work days, and for the newest of the nation's finest, you get used to the ideal that daylight is down time. Well, on behalf of the spouses that are usually fed up with sleeping alone, we try to either stay up all day and sleep with them at night. Sometimes we sleep a couple of hours, get up when we're really in that heavy sleep (yeah, right) and then try to go back to sleep like "normal people." At least give us the credit that we do try, at least at times.

Now, put in part time jobs as an additional factor that dictates our sleeping pattern and you can see how hard it is to please, even when we try.

I think many cops think of a day off as a reason to play hermit for a day. Every little task requested becomes so monumental, even something as trivial as taking out the trash, is a task worthy of a congressional directive. Any request, whether valid (in our eyes) or not, is such an imposition that even getting out of our favorite chair should result in nasty stares, heavy sighs and usually a snotty, "Is it a problem if I sit down for a minute on *MY* day off?"

To the wives and husbands of cops, we really don't want to be as tacky as we sound. We're being very selfish, for our own well being if you can believe that, and if it hasn't been said before, and on behalf of all of us, I'm sorry. And yes, despite our actions, we do love you very, very much.

Well, now let's look at the myriad of other things commonly associated with a day off. For starters, the yard. Few things drain me quicker than the prospect of starting the lawn mower. It takes but a few hours but, though defense lawyers rank right up there with dentists, I'd rather give myself a root canal than pull that nasty cord that starts a weed eater.

It's kinda like crime. If I mow the yard to a pristine beauty worthy of Buckingham Palace, in a few weeks it needs it all over again. If I clear the streets of all the crime that would dare grow in my neighborhood, in a few weeks, if not constantly attended to, it all grows back. Even thicker than it was before I first mowed it.

In other words, it can't be ignored and it will never cease to need attention.

If I had a dollar for every time I told my wife to just wait for this or that, to get done, until my days off. It's not until I read my own writing that I begin to understand why my wife didn't seem to think my having a "day off" would solve the world's problems. She's been there, done that and nobody, but nobody, can procrastinate and sound as thoroughly convincing as can a cop.

Let's take this week, for example and like I said before, this is true stuff. I got off Sunday morning at about 0730am and, after shedding my armor, I wake up my unintentionally spoiled sweetie to prepare her for church. At about 9ish she's on her way and I do a few chores and relax, for a moment. I can't help but think of the week that's coming and I'm just now starting my precious days off.

On Monday I'll be teaching at the police academy (for free) and, not only is it raining now, but it's gonna rain tomorrow night when I teach our newest of the best how to safely effect felony stops, at night. Yeah, get real wet, for four or five hours, on your day off, with the only driving factor being a desire to get our future cop's home at night, to their families, the same ones that I'm neglecting on my day off to make it a reality.

Well, I've done it (taught at the academy, this is where I started typing again), got drenched and even talked one of our new officers in joining me. I almost felt guilty at first, after all, he's not getting paid either and nobody, but nobody, needs money more than the family of a new police officer.

I'm glad I didn't feel guilty. It was, by the way, his day off too, and, when I stopped to pick him up, he was in the living room with his wife, feeding their darling infant. He springs to his feet, covers his heart with Kevlar and off we go. I'll say this and it's very, very important.

She didn't bat an eye, in fact she even offered support, asking only when he'd be home so dinner would be ready. God bless her and please give her the strength to keep understanding where his devotion for helping others doesn't diminish his love for his family, the one's he really doing the job for.

Well, we're home and, due to the rain, those devoted few veterans in uniform that on a clear day said they'd be glad to be there, they stayed in their warm and dry homes. We show up and the academy coordinator looks like he just passed a kidney stone.

Turns out, only one (of about a dozen) showed up and our newest officer gets a real quick course in teaching others. Three felony car scenarios and only one instructor, prior to our arrival. By the way, he did great. He had no choice and he wouldn't have it any other way. He wears a uniform for a reason and that reason was never clearer than when we walked into the classroom.

I can't resist this opportunity. How many white collar suit dwellers here would stand in the rain, for no money, on your day off, with your family at home, with you're only driving force to help others in your field?

Answer. That's why you put on cuff links, collar stays and a tie clip and why we put on a badge.

I meant to tell a "typical" cop's day off but this has turned into my days off, this week. Well, it still works, for I'm just beginning. I have tomorrow, which consists of my promise to take my daughter to the mall for Hanson books, to go to our tax man, to drop by wife's employer (she's in a c-collar), then go to a Fraternal Order of Police meeting.

On the following two days I'll be in a distant part of the state learning how to be a police "manager" and, yet again, I'll spend a day off away from the family, this time in a motel room with other officer's neglecting their families.

Well, I should be back on my last day off. The problem is, upon my return, I'm due at two places, at the same time. Check that, at three places, at the same time. I'm supposed to do something I really love, which is, to talk to the first time drunk driving offenders and pray that just one hears my sincerity. The second meeting (at the same time) is a lecture at one of our local public schools.

Problem is, I found out about my upcoming speech from a thank-you letter from the school and, in as much as I read the letter from my mailbox at work, I had absolutely no idea I was supposed to be there. Thirdly, and most important, and you quick one's already guessed it, my cherished family.

Sadly ironic, but sure to come, is that for the one I please I've not only offended the other two by my absence but I've tarnished my department. Like I said about ten chapters ago. If you try to please em' all you'll go nuts and if you stop trying to, you've lost the edge that makes it so important for you to so carefully polish your badge each night.

One last comment on days off and I'll drive on. If cops, or lawyers, or teachers, welders, or every occupation from astronaut to nuclear physicist, if each would truly enjoy a day off, and not think of how quick it ends but how to enjoy it when it's here, we'd all be much happier.

Every living being can have their breath taken as quickly as the blink of an eye. I know. I've seen it. Usually, the end has come from a traffic accident. After all, we're heading somewhere, a set destination, and just that quickly I'm dispatched to a wreck, preparing for the worst.

You're right, not an accident call will be heard by my ears that I don't think of the "old" reserve days and the lifeless body of that legless child. I've seen what seems like a zillion lost limbs and dead bodies since then, but that one will never fade. I have little doubt that if those, whose time had come, yet, knew it was coming, how their actions prior to that final breath would have taken a far different course.

Maybe all of us could learn from the misfortunes of others and live for today how we should have lived yesterday, had we only known. Lord, please give me the strength and ability to practice what I preach!

By the way, in the last chapter, I spoke for a minute about being promoted a cop supervisor. To end this chapter is fitting for the chapter that proceeded it, specifically, that once promoted not a day off goes by that the office doesn't call with a problem or a member of your shift calls asking for a little time off. Not so much for a day off, but for some time off.

The biggest and probably most obvious problem is, if you (supervisor) give them the time off or if they are granted the time off, both will be thinking of the troops at work, really.

What if that night, that you took off, resulted in a fellow officer falling (forever), or getting hurt, or calls were stacked up and the citizens we live for had to wait too long for an officer to respond? Somebody is either hurt, killed, or at least neglected, all because we wanted to spend a little time with the family, to regroup, to make up for all those shifts we worked diligently, and our family couldn't sleep because we were. Yes sir, yes ma'am, it is a no win day off, if you allow it to be.

Don't think for a second we don't ask the good Lord to ride shotgun, either with us or because of our absence, though it matters not if they believe in the Almighty. I promise if it really goes bad on a shift or on a day off, He's the first one they'll want to get to know. I've seen it happen again and again, and if they were a true non-believer, they seem to be the most sincere of all. It's hard to explain in words, so I won't even try.

CHAPTER THIRTEEN
From A Recruit's Eyes

Got a joke/question for you. What's the difference between God and a cop? (I heard this one from an attorney).

God doesn't think he's a cop.

In a way, though admittedly humorous, there are several things in that joke that actually hit very close to home. Yes, some cops do think they're "Almighty." I hope that every future cop feels they're invincible yet possess the common sense to know they're not. The good Lord knows what lies ahead, we don't.

It's a sad fact that many, many police officers who are killed in the line of duty are from their own firearms. If not from the stress that leads to suicide, it's the result of losing a hands-on battle in the streets.

Now, look at every recruit trying to qualify on the firing range, to earn the opportunity to be a cop, yet, you realize how possible it is that the very gun they hold in their hands may result in their own death. Believe me, every range-master knows it, but to even broach the subject at this crucial, early part of their career would result in a recruit that will be too paranoid to serve the public. In 1996 alone, four police officers were shot with their own service weapons.

It's one of those things that you would learn in the academy that would, for many, not only encompass every field contact but, eventually, lead some to "hide" behind the badge and not to live for it. When the badge is used for a shield of protection and not for a shield of honor, they're back to pushing dental floss, and realistically, this is not an uncommon scenario.

In 1996, on May 23rd , an off-duty officer with the Dayton Police Department was shot and killed as he was reporting for his shift. The 25-year-old member of the nation's finest, in the company of another off-duty officer, were about to enter their district headquarters when a male approached them from behind who made a sound at them.

As the officers turned toward him, he opened fire with a 9mm handgun. Initially hitting the victim officer in the hand and knocking him to the ground, the assailant then shot the second officer in the face, knocking him down also. He then leaned over the first officer, who was wearing body armor, and shot him in the head. Fellow officers, responding to the gunfire, shot and killed the 24-year-old assailant.

The victim officer, that had worked so hard to become a cop, enjoyed 4 months in uniform. A true recruit and officer in every sense of the word. He didn't die stopping a stolen car, or chasing a robbery suspect, or even handling a domestic disturbance or saving a drunk driver from coating our streets with blood. He was killed walking to work, hoping only to help any and all who would summon his expertise. Yes, to help the very one that struck him down, and he'd have been happy to respond.

I've changed the beginning of this chapter about a dozen times. So many things are about to fill the souls of our future crime fighters that I found it hard it tell what future experience should encompass the opening paragraph of this chapter.

How do you tell an academy recruit that, if assigned to the day shift on a hot summer day, he'll have to use his/her lunch break to change their sweat laden uniforms for a one that won't offend the public? That is, of course, if the recruit does his job and doesn't hide at the office or in their air-conditioned cruiser. (Yes, Mark, I admit to hiding when you fingerprinted that stolen car on 5th street, August '98.)

You can't believe the heat that builds from behind a vest, with the water that once filled your cells soaking that tee shirt that must be gleamingly white. For those officers that hide and feel that the city they serve owes them a living, I'll be as brutally honest about them as I will the defense (lawyers). I've settled for this little story to start their careers.

Every single cop, in their early days, will have an experience that is so harsh, so real, that they question the path they've chosen and they really get scared. I mean a deep down, unbelievable, give you the cold sweat can't sleep for a week fear. Mine was in my early reserve days and I promise you it will never fade. Please hang with me till I'm done.

I was working the midnight shift with a Cherokee County deputy sheriff and, just before midnight, we check on what's happened on the previous shift and take a head count of the prisoners. Well, the earlier events were passed on and, prior to hitting the county gravel roads, we check on the prisoners.

The cell blocks are divided into two separate areas, divided by a cinder block wall. One is for the male population and the other, for the ladies that opted for an easier way to excel. Well, the men were all there, some happy to visit with us and the others threatening to blow up everything from our house to our cat's litter box.

Once the head count is finished, we have a juvenile male to check on that can't for legal reasons be held with the adults housed in the ladies side. The deputy walks in first, immediately runs out and screams, to the lone dispatcher, "Signal-thirty."

As he flies by me, I look in the cell and see a fifteen-year-old boy, hanging from his shoelaces, tied to the top of a shower pipe. Though I would see a stadium full of dead bodies in the decade to follow, none will ever hit me more than this one did, not even the gut-wrenching lifelessness of the infant's leg.

He was dressed only in shorts and his entire torso, from waist up, was as white as a hospital sheet. His legs were solid purple, his eyes were protruding from their sockets and his tongue was as thick as a pork-chop.

Something else I've never seen before, or since, was a line of spit. It started from the corner of his mouth, was as thin as a string, but it went on and on for about 10 inches. Straight as an arrow, almost like an icicle. He just hung there, void of life, and inch for inch and pound for pound, he could have been my double in a uniform.

I have never, ever, been so close to death and felt it at the same time. I realized then that my uniform didn't make me invincible and it was startling how soon I thought I could die how quickly it could happen.

I went outside, by the exercise yard and just looked out, not at anything in particular, just away from the cell that accepted the life of that child.

There was something exceptionally morose about that death. Many veteran officers filed in, one by one, to gaze at the dead body (all cops do it, I'll not try to explain further). They've seen countless deaths. Many make jokes about it in an attempt, in their eyes, to maintain their sanity, to be the tough cop.

But even these guys were visibly shaken, in fact, one even got sick. I still don't understand it. They've seen broken bodies, shattered bones, shoulders missing their heads, countless rivers of blood, name it. But this one, missing all those expected adjectives associated with death, this one hit home with everybody.

While I was standing outside, trying to understand the feelings a "real cop" isn't supposed to feel, I felt a hand on my shoulder and found the sheriff at my side. I started to tell him I was fine, that he could count on me for any situation, but he stopped me before I got started.

He'd been there. A mountain of a man, huge in both size and respect given him by the citizens. He said, "It doesn't get easier, it never will, but, you'll find your own way to deal with it. If I could tell you how to deal with it, I'd be the Man upstairs, not the sheriff." He was right.

If you could bottle the sincerity and pure drive that feeds every cell of a man or woman that just got confirmation they were accepted for employment, for the first time, at a law enforcement agency, a fart would resemble a nuclear bomb. It's that potent and I wish I could be around when they really find out what they've just gotten themselves into.

It's wonderful at times yet the epitome of frustration on a routine basis. Oh, how I wish I had the ability to be at every single one of their sides, when they feel their first cop hurt and I could place the Band-aid of past experience on the wounds of the unavoidable pains that are certain to replay, at least for a while, every time their heads hit the pillow.

Our future, as far as sleeping well and trusting that our lives won't be violated, is dependent on the cops of tomorrow. In the police academy, they will learn to reconstruct an accident with the tenacity that our kids will learn their multiplication tables in elementary school. It's symbolic of learning anew to read, write, spell, even walk. Everything is brand new to police recruits, and at least before the system or co-workers are allowed to corrupt them, they are genuine in their desire to serve, to clean up the streets.

I remember my first day at the police academy as clear as yesterday. Unfortunately, yesterday was a really long day. Symbolic of my first day in junior high, and high school, and college, I was the smallest one there, but I'm used to that. They'll get to know me so that wasn't a concern.

Every new recruit at the academy is a child at heart and that's but one reason why we need the best of the best to be willing to trade the field for a classroom. The problem is for the money (we do have to have it, after all, though it's not our driving force) everyone put in, an academy instructor position could make more money working as a security guard.

Again, this is where our desire to live our goals overtakes our desire to have stocks and bonds. And, believe it or not, we might wonder where we could have been, but, we don't regret the path we've chosen (at least, not on a regular basis).

With no disrespect to the abilities of our academy dwellers of the future, a police recruit looks for support and discipline symbolic of the drive behind the huge eyes of a puppy in the pet shop window. They want only to be protected, nurtured and taught right from wrong, whether they know it at that time or not. If you teach a puppy that doodling on the carpet is okay, they obviously won't respect the carpet they walk on. If you smack their nose with newspaper when they do wrong, they learn not only a respect for property and respect for you, but respect for themselves.

If we teach our police recruits to respect others, from personal feelings to the property and beliefs of others, and find a way to ensure that respect never "burns out," if that's possible, we've done very well.

When I finished the police academy, my field training consisted of four hours in a police car with a sergeant pointing out buildings, streets and away I was sent. After all, fresh out of the academy, I knew it all, right?

Hardly.

The academy teaches you the basics but only two things will keep you healthy and afford you the opportunity to "visit" your neglected family at the end of a shift. Those two elements are simply, common sense and street experience. It's that simple yet one without the other will not ever, ever, result in a law enforcement career, at least one to be proud of, that will make our children proud of us or avoid the services of a $1,200 suit on retainer.

It's my understanding that the average length of a police academy, which is inclusive of both private and state academies, is approximately twelve weeks long.

Ideally, a police academy should begin in the classroom and end with our first retirement check. That's in a perfect world, with all the right motivators, and frankly, we ain't there.

Realistically, we never will be. That's actually good in a way. If all were the same we'd be robots, not people. And it takes people, not machinery, to respect feelings and to have not only the ability but also the sensitivity to be a cop.

A human robot, that bleeds when cut yet reacts with the speed of a Pentium chip, will be the only answer to ensuring the safety and well being of our cop's of tomorrow. Problem is, it's not practical. The tears that we commonly shed on the "inside" (you'll probably never see them) would surely short out a robot.

If the average police academy is twelve weeks long, then six weeks should be spent on the basic skills and six weeks would be mental preparation. In six weeks, I can teach you what to do, properly, with the body parts of a killed child.

Do you think a twelve week academy, or even a twelve year academy, could teach you how to deal with the prospect of knowing next year, or next week, or even that your next call might send you to another lifeless limb. Most importantly, and where I'm heading with this, is how on earth do you teach a future crime-fighter to prepare for a body part at six o'clock and then to deal with a citizen with their keys locked in their car at six-thirty? And don't forget to smile when you arrive at the scene (they don't want to know where you've been).

Remember, the puppy dog eyes and total virginity of cop life yet to come are dependant on your words, and you'd damn well better mean every one for you can rest assured the recruits won't forget them. I wish I had a nickel, strike that you money loving $1,200 suits, I wish I had an extra day on earth for every time I said, "We never learned this S**t in the academy!"

Let me stress again what I said just a few lines ago. How do you mentally prepare a future cop to wake up each day, and enthusiastically look and act as professional as the movies depict us, yet realize that call after call after call, day after day after day, each could summon our response to death, or body parts, never having the luxury of a few days (that's a weekend to you normal M-F, 9-5 folks)

126

to regroup?

Remember something here. We, those that teach the cops of tomorrow (I do it on my own time), know what's coming in their future but how on earth do we tell them what to expect, if that's possible, yet not understand or blame them if they flee from the room screaming.

Let's get back to the basics, after all, it's the basic police academy. You'll learn of felony car stops, domestic disturbances, accident investigation, finding the laws in volumes of texts, that we will enforce daily, death notifications (like you can learn that in a classroom), crime scenes, shooting a gun, writing a report, dealing with crime victims, on and on.

We're taught basic first aid but every veteran cop will warn of the dangers of giving the breath of life to one gasping for our attention. If you can ignore their pleas, and sleep at the end of your day's work, you better find comfort in a $1,200 suit because you might fit in a uniform but you'll never earn it, or hang it with pride, in your closet, much less wear it with dignity on our streets.

There is one constant, in every academy, that will serve you well on the streets you will soon work. You'll get used to being to told how to do your job. The instructors will tell you in the academy and the citizens will tell you when you make a traffic stop, even for the simplest of infractions.

One huge difference that our occupation has over others that we'll deal with is as follows. If I stop a banker, I couldn't begin to tell him how to accrue interest annually, must less how to amortize what I don't have. If I stop a school teacher I couldn't begin to correctly place every state capitol on an empty map of this, the best nation on Earth.

If I stop a surgeon I couldn't replace his mitral-valve nor could I "legally" and appropriately file a writ of Habeus Corpus if I stop an attorney. I can say though, through experience, that every one of the occupations above have told me or one my cohorts of mercy how to do our job, though I'd have loved to have seen them try, but without the benefit of a desk to retreat to, much less an office door to lock behind you.

Yes, I have been brutally honest (or cruel to some) on lawyers, strike that, defense lawyers. I wish I could find a defense attorney willing to speak to a basic police academy. I would dare say that all would support their vigorously pursuing the intoxicated driver, especially the first time offender. That's guaranteed money in the bank for, with the nauseating fee they charge to reduce your crime, the courts will do for free. That's standard practice, quid pro quo, if you will.

Not only do they (the defense) tell you that you need not appear for court, that they'll represent your best interest, they don't want you in court. Might give away an inside secret, and that means a delayed payment on their summer villa. Pity.

One of the most beneficial lessons in understanding the public, for a new recruit, would be in the courtroom, but not one of their own cases. I would love to have a recruit witness a crime, while off-duty, observe the officer's actions, the suspect actions and then follow it up with a court appearance. A mouthy or aggressive drunk driver would suffice.

Without being personally involved, they would see the reason for the stop, hopefully not involving the frequent pain involved, just a "routine" drunk driver. They blame "the cop" for everything and, when the State's test confirms they're drunk, the machine is almost always "broken," or it was remembering the "real drunk" that was tested before. After hours of verbal, and/or physical abuse, then they start their report, still trying to reflect the utmost of professionalism.

To make this quick, we follow them to court, and my, what a transformation. The drunk driver not only has an expected memory lapse of his actions but ooh how proud he is that men and women would be willing to wear a badge and protect the citizens of such a fine, loving, law abiding community. And by the way, he/she doesn't mind the inconvenience of an over zealous officer "hauling" them to jail, even though they only had two glasses of wine with dinner.

To end this daily, no, hourly scenario, he/she is told not to let it happen again and, boom, free again, usually with a conviction far less than originally guilty of, sorry suits, alleged to have committed. Never mind that they'd have kicked our ass when we brought them in, if, of course, we weren't wearing that uniform and badge. Of course, though, when we take the handcuffs off, they forgot all about the threats to harm us, brought on by their beer muscles, and they leave their threats to a lawsuit for the "excessive force" they endured while rubbing the marks on their wrists as a result of being in handcuffs.

And by the way, as a rule, we don't handcuff you for our protection, it's to protect you from us, as a result of the actions you might not otherwise take if you were not under the influence of a substance. Besides, it's policy at every department I've ever known, so don't flatter yourself. Be content the next day with telling all your buddies how it took five of us to bring you in. Odds are, at least one of those ears in your social group will read through the lines, if not from experience, from common sense.

This is a scene they'll play out a thousand times over, and if they experience it without it being "personal," maybe the care they feel for the public, every time a handcuff is secured, will tell them that they did do a good job, that they did make a difference, at least that night. That little bit of understanding will ensure they polish their boots and belt buckle for the shift yet to follow, when their heads hit the understanding of a pillow.

A very important lesson for the recruits of tomorrow, and I'll try to be brief, is to prepare them for the "experience" that they will receive at the hands of veteran officers and supervisors, not by actions, but by words. The best thing I can say, and listen closely, is to hear every word uttered, ridiculous or not, to you at the time, but hear them all.

You'll learn what was good to hear and through the years, you'll learn what to listen to. Somehow, through the years, you'll be able to grow as an officer, and often that may come from the negative ramblings of the department's laziest veteran cop or at least in your opinion at the time, the least respected supervisor who never earned your respect.

Even if their words were wrong, and you realize it later, you've learned not to say, or do, what you once heard them say. It happens to me every day and expect to lower your ego enough to realize, years later, they may have actually been right on track. There's a lot to learn from long timers and most of it is good and will help keep you healthy on those mean streets. As long as you listen, prior to judging, you'll be way ahead of the game.

A huge part of the incidents recruit officers will deal with, in their probationary year, will involve to some degree people under the influence of an intoxicant. That much they'll learn and grow to expect. In a way, that's fitting.

Beer is brewed, whiskey is distilled, wine is aged and water purified. Those are natural processes that are expected to yield a certain product. A recruit cop is aged, hopefully to ripe old age, by experience and common sense. That isn't an expected process, for it never ends and we'll never know how our product of the academy will handle the challenges that follow, with every single breath, every time they polish their shield of honor.

One last item and we'll move on. As is equal with all professions, yes, even lawyers, you (the recruit) will get out of the academy what you put into it. These personal work ethics will dictate every career and ultimately when you last see your badge on an engraved plaque, these ethics will determine whether it was a career of honor, or just a job.

I'll say it again. If it is just a job, then hunt elsewhere, for it won't be a career. It'll be a meager paycheck, with constant gripes, turmoil, let-downs and, most likely, will never result in a retirement party where you're handed that plaque. You can no longer just exist in the law enforcement world of today. You will benefit society and dispense justice with authoritative care, or you'll not survive.

I said I was moving on, but, I can't leave here just yet, at least not until I get a chance to gripe about some personal observations and then, hopefully, put it all together to explain why my feelings hopefully will open your eyes to us.

I have been a die-hard Chicago Cubbie's fan since I moved to Oklahoma and had the juice to the cable turned on. I began to know every player, every stat, heck I'd even plan my sleep around the next game. If "Ryno" (Sandberg) struck out, I got an ulcer right along with him. If the soon to be legendary, Hall-of-Famer Mark Grace missed a play at first, I was there to offer my support, at least in spirit.

Well, to make a long, personal frustration short, I began rooting for Greg Maddux. He had the youth to be around forever and the talent to re-write the books. Well, after a typically great season, and being awarded the Cy Young award, the City of Chicago couldn't wait to see Greg grace the pitcher's mound at Wrigley Field for many years to come.

Well, at twenty-nothing years old, and being offered twenty-something million-plus dollars, he says, to the effect, no, I want twenty-something-plus-and-then-some million dollars. More money than he could ever spend in his grandkids' lifetimes was already lining his pockets, but he had to have more.

Most of us manage to feed, shelter and clothe our families on less money in a year than he'll earn for one inning's *work* (yeah), but it wasn't enough. No loyalty, no devotion, no care for the city that treated him as their own. The end result, of course, is that he went to Atlanta and lived happily ever after, except of course, for the City of Chicago that he so callously betrayed. One year after the almighty dollar bought his soul, he returned to Chicago, but this time as an opponent. I'll never forget the response.

One of the most fortunate people on earth, that God gave a special talent and he was literally booed off the field. It was not out of disrespect for his abilities, but out of disgust that he could so quickly turn his back on those that considered him family.

You, the recruit, have the same expectations of loyalty to and from your respective communities that Mr. Maddux *had* with the Chicago fans. Actually, you (the recruit) have more expected of your talents. If Maddux has a bad game, he'll go home to his mansion and pick out from a long line of those he'll allow to kiss his ass or bless their existence with an autograph. If a twenty-nothing year-old cop has a bad night, they're either out of a job, sued, disciplined, transferred or staring at their own mahogany pitcher's mound, if they're lucky.

One other very important difference between the spoiled Maddux's you (the recruit) will deal with on the street and what he (Greggy) takes for granted. We don't have the luxury of several Cy Young awards resting on our mantle that make many National League umpires (too many) afford him a strike zone the size of many commercial vehicles, yet, they still give him credit. The talent is still there, but, sadly, the dollars won't allow the fans to ever see it again, unless it's in his (present) home town, or they have no idea how quickly he can (has) turn on those that feed his family.

The obvious difference, that is by now quite clear, is that many folks live for money but none I assure you wear a uniform, well, short of a baseball jersey. I'll be this honest. I never have, nor ever will, possess the ability to throw a baseball with the skill of Greg Maddux. By the same token, based on my personal knowledge of the degree of honesty, integrity, ethics and devotion required to be a professional police officer in today's streets, and my personal feelings of those talents obviously not possessed by Greg Maddux, he never had the heart to live life behind the badge. I guess you're not the only one that possesses the ability to strike one out, Mr. Maddux.

I guess that makes me and Mr. Maddux even in numbers, but I feel I'm far ahead in the pride that I have telling folks not only what I do for a living, but where I do it and where our (the nation's finest of the future) driving force's lie.

I can also, unlike Mr. Maddux, look my daughter in the eyes and tell her I work for a living to *help* others, every single day and I truly do make a difference. No, not in the checkbook (which is obviously where his motivation lies) but in the knowledge that I'm doing everything I can to ensure a safe and secure living room for every baseball fan of tomorrow.

CHAPTER FOURTEEN
The Death Penalty

Absolutely.

CHAPTER FIFTEEN
To Bury A Cop

This one might take me a while to start, much less to finish, so please be patient. Over 14,000 names of the silent few that cared enough to die for the families they've never known will be etched for eternity onto the dark gray walls of the National Law Enforcement Memorial Wall. Lord, what a sickening and sad day for the engravers on-duty September 11th.

You have to travel to Washington, D.C. to see this monument, yet ironically, you need only to travel a few blocks to visit with the same group of public servants that, before they've earned that respect, at least in the eyes of the public, are still alive to offer you their utmost, every single hour of every single day.

Please allow me to give you a few facts that come directly from the U.S. Department of Justice. Since 1987, nearly 700 law enforcement officers have been slain, another 696 killed in duty-related accidents, and over 600,000 assaulted.

In 1996, 53 of 55 slayers of law enforcement officers have been cleared. Of the 74 suspects identified in connection with the murders (that's not a fair fight, even in a parking lot), 72 were male, 1 was female and gender was not reported for 1. Thirty-one of the suspects were white and thirty-three were black. Fifty-four of the 74 alleged assailants were under the age of 31 (no wonder we take juvenile crimes and threats seriously).

One last statement from the Department of Justice and I'll go with my feelings. Among those persons charged with killing a cop for whom the final disposition is known, 72 percent were found guilty of murder; 9 percent were found guilty of a lesser offense related to murder; and 5 percent were found guilty of some crime other than murder. Nine percent of the suspects were acquitted or had charges against them dismissed, and 2 percent were committed to psychiatric institutions.

If you think a cop doesn't have feelings, doesn't really care about a life other than their own, can't cry, just go to the funeral of a cop. I've been to far too many, and though none were a co-worker, at least not in the sense of knowing him/her personally, when they were shot, stabbed, clubbed, beaten, blown up or tortured, all those that wear a badge bled.

At first, you go out of respect, but once you're there, you know it's family. You try not to look in the faces of the fallen officer's fellow officers, for you know a tear is slowly falling. And it's almost impossible to look at the families of the officer that died. It's too close to home, too possible that your family is seated on the front row and those in attendance are there out of respect for what you chose to do for a living.

I've been to a funeral with a fellow officer and it was a member of his family, actually, his mother. I knew he was crying inside but I never saw a tear. About a year later, I was standing at his side during the funeral of an officer that was shot to death in a city about two-hundred miles away.

When "Taps" played, and the folded American Flag was presented to the cop's widow, he began to shake and the tears flew like rain. It's hard to explain, short of, that every time a police officer is laid to rest, and his/her department vigilantly stands at attention, clenching their jaws, trying in vain to maintain that professional appearance, a part of every officer lies inside that coffin. Forever.

Let me tell you a little about attending the funeral of a police officer, actually, of a public servant. If you scan the seas of uniforms that are in attendance, it's not limited to gun belts and bullet proof vests. You'll see fire fighters, paramedics, dispatchers, troopers, game wardens, clergy, citizens, even convenience store clerks (in uniform).

The tie that binds the non-public servants is respect and the tie that bands public servants warrants the title of this book. The badge. You put one on and your family just grew by about a million, inclusive of every occupant of your neighborhood police station, fire house and the back of every ambulance.

I made a tape of the funeral of a Tulsa police officer that was shot to death, in the line of duty and, regardless how many times I watch it, it's still never the same. I was in attendance, along with officers from about every state, neighboring or not, including Canada. This officer, with a physical size equaled only by his compassion for the public, was shot in his head as he walked back to his patrol car. He knew it could happen, yet, he never knew that it did.

When his fellow officers spoke of his greatness, their voices cracked, just like the trumpeters in uniform that couldn't hit the high notes while respectfully playing "Taps," thinking only of their fallen comrade with each breath that filled the trumpet mouthpiece.

At least six people that stood at attention around me, for hours, fell to the ground, due to both the scorching heat and the emotions that they attempted to hold back. Without a word said, and for a reason that I can't quite explain, only those that were necessary came to their aid and the others standing around them remained at attention, despite it being all we've ever lived for to rush to those in need.

One scene I never hope to be a part off, for I'd never see it (at least in person) would be for my wife and daughter to be presented with the flag we've sworn to uphold. It would be placed in their laps, under the shield of a cemetery tent, with the chief of police having the honor, and to a degree the blame, of trying to explain why it was for a good reason.

If any person on this planet can place the folded American flag in the lap of a small child, tell them why mommy or daddy has gone to heaven and then sleep that night, I'd hate to meet you. Actually, I probably have met you, but I guarantee you weren't wearing a uniform and, most likely, if our paths did cross, you were in the back seat of my police car, or running from it.

Something else that is distinctive about the funeral of a police officer. Despite the fact that officers from everywhere are present, you'll never see the family member of a cop present, unless, they were close to the fallen officer's family. In other words, police spouses and families aren't invited, but you never have to explain the reason why and they'll never ask.

For the officers, it's because you've spent your whole life shielding them from this very scenario.

For the spouses and family members, they know this is about as painful as your life gets, and it's obvious without you ever having to say a word. They don't ask to go and you don't invite them. Maybe they're afraid they'll see you cry or maybe they're afraid they will see themselves on the front row, with all those in uniform unable to look you in the eyes.

Allow me to pose a question to the defense lawyers out there, yes, the $1,200 suits. How many times do you drink that first cup of coffee in the morning and know, by proven statistics, that before you enjoy a cup the following morning that a fellow member of your profession has been has been killed, at the hands of the public, the same ones you'll be happy (or forced) to defend?

Heck, you'll look for what the dead guy (officer) did wrong just to free the one you've sworn to defend, and you'll say it's for justice. If you're a public defender, and have no choice but to defend, then do your job, but don't bring discredit to ours.

For the Italian suits, if you take the case by choice, at least do us the justice of attending the officer's funeral and, please, if humanity and care hasn't been purchased by your broker, look at the folded flag in the lap of the mourning children. As each tender tear falls past their innocent cheek, look at the cheeks of your client and, with God as your witness, do what's right.

Before you defend your client at least show respect for the families that are forced to live behind the badge that will now only yield memories. I pray that you think of every ticket they've written, every call they've responded to, every dead body, every dead or crying neglected child, every accident, every fight, every time they were summoned to help. That includes locking your keys in your car, barking dogs, snakes on your patio, aliens in your attic, you name it.

Every "client" we've responded to we did out of concern, unlike you. We can't pick and choose what calls to take, in other words, to handle only the wealthy and clean. We take what we get, we go where we're told to and you don't have the choice of selecting whom you'll "serve and protect."

All in the controlled setting of your office complete with highback leather chairs and desks worthy of a CEO, including a telephone to call the police if you feel threatened.

Our office is the street, our chairs are car seats and, if we lose a client, we're either sued or our family gets a rectangular flag, placed delicately in their laps. Now, if you can look at my fellow brothers and sisters in uniform with contempt, while sitting in a courtroom, away from our families and tell us how poorly we did our jobs, you are a truly sick bastard, yet, you and your client are the very reason our profession will always be in demand.

If you can do it, and sleep well, your suit just went from $1,200 to $2,500, and you actually get to fly to Italy to get it. If you have the guts, tell the tailor how you managed to afford it.

Even more, if you're a real man or woman sworn to serve justice, in the safe attire of a defense lawyer, do me a favor. While in Italy, or France, or Neiman Marcus, take a second, after you put on that swell looking suit and go visit the grave of a fallen cop.

If you're willing to make the time, find his/her family and tell them that your clients are of the same breed that you just got freed on a technicality, that is, if you defended a cop killer.

When an officer falls, we, those that have ever worn a uniform or hung a badge from our belt, cover the center of our badge with a thin piece of black material. It symbolizes that an officer has died and we'll wear it on our badge until the day of the funeral. For just a few days, it is a constant reminder that the number of select few, devoted souls that protect you has just gotten a little smaller.

When we take the material off, we place it in a drawer, knowing full well that we'll have to wear it again, stand at attention for a while and hear "Taps" moan, all while unsuccessfully holding back our tears, again trying to block our families from our thoughts.

It's scenes like this, that we sadly know will be repeated, that make it all but impossible to remember the triumphs during our careers. The lost kids that we returned home, the dying that maybe got a chance to breath again, the smoke that we spotted falling from your rooftops while you innocently and unknowingly slept inside. All highlights, both at the time and in our retirement years, yet strangely forgotten as the endless line of police cars escorts yet another fallen comrade to their final resting place.

Folks, I imagine I could find a well known author to make it all seem poetic, but life isn't always poetry.

CHAPTER SIXTEEN
Some Final Thoughts

I'll tell you, America, the land of the free, what we need from today's law enforcement professionals.

We need White policemen, and White policewomen.

We need Black policemen, and Black policewomen.

We need Asian policemen; we need Asian police women.

We need Hispanic policemen; we need Hispanic policewomen.

We need Indian policemen; we need Indian policewomen.

We need Jewish policemen; we need Jewish policewomen.

We need Amish, Chinese, Iranians and Egyptians, Hillbillies, Canadian, Russian and, well, every nationality or nickname that has a nation or group they call home, and, if America is now theirs, that's what we need in today's rank and file squad room.

The true beauty of where I'm headed with this is when we begin to see the law enforcement officer, in other words the badge and not the color of their skin, we'll be on our way.

I have a request of every soul that cared enough to not only start reading this book, but to make it this far. I'll leave an address at the end of this book with the sincere hope (really) that you'll tell me of your experiences with the law dogs. Good, bad, caring or crude, I do want your input. It's through the citizens that we serve that we learn how to grow, not only as police officers, but also as citizens ourselves. By the way, for the defense attorneys out there that send me a package, yes, I will dunk it in water, eat lunch and then listen your comments. By the way, if I send it back unopened, would you re-open it?

As I read, and re-read, the words that I've written, this tells of my soul but certainly doesn't give you an idea of the humor I commonly enjoy nor the respect for others that I cherish. My intent was not to be as serious as the words in this book displays, but I guess that I couldn't poetically steer clear of how serious the job of living the life of a uniformed public servant is in today's world.

I love nothing more than my family, which is led by my wife and daughter, thanks solely to the values instilled into me by my parents and reinforced to this day. My mother has been a constant ally that I love, and respect, much more than I tell her. My father and brother have my utmost love and respect and I'm truly a better person for having been blessed with their unconditional love. True, they are professionals in every sense of the word, even down to the high dollar suits. The big difference with the suits they wear versus the ones I've constantly referred to is simple. They never harmed a soul, mentally or otherwise, to afford the appearance they've rightfully earned, that is publicly expected. Both knew the direction they wanted to go and they fought their way to achieve it. They earned not only the right to wear that suit, and the collegiate degrees to afford those suits, but most importantly and the big difference here is that they never used the misfortunes of others to pay for it.

To those offended by my words that may have scorched your egos, I guess I should apologize, *to a degree.* To label all lawyers clad in $1,200 suits as the bad guys is as unfair as saying all cops possess the honesty and ethics of Mark Furman. I'll give you that much, and as I said earlier, if your true pursuit of justice is sincere, then wear that $150 suit, from the rack, with pride, for you've earned every thread. For the lawyers and suit dwellers with whom my words mirrored your driving force, I hope a glass of ice water in hell comes to mind if you're in search of an apology from me.

First and foremost, to all the past, present and future public servants of these, our streets, I offer my most sincere thanks. You have done, are doing or will soon do what only a handful can and only you can truly understand the career you've chosen. I pray nightly that it's filled with more joy than pain, more satisfaction than frustration. I'll counter to what I've already said before. At times you can't for the life of you understand why you've chosen this path, yet, if you could do it all over again, and this time you knew what was coming, I'll lay odds you'd still follow step for step the exact same trail.

And, with all the love I've ever known, I want to thank the supportive families that have allowed us to wear that uniform every day and night. For every material item we couldn't afford to offer you, though you're so much more deserving in many ways than the spouses of bread winners that took the clean and easy way out, that received the things you should have, please find some comfort with the fact that we would have had it only been possible.

You've patiently slept alone, looked at the luxury cars with personalized license tags while you struggled to get your domestic, affordable car started and we thank you. From the mink coats that will never grace your shoulders and the center kitchen island that you'll only see in a magazine, we thank you. From the diamond solitaires that were replaced with cubic zirconia baubles or diamond chips that had to accented with silver backgrounds, we all thank you. From the weekends you shopped alone or for the miles you've walked carrying in the groceries or carrying out the trash, which is our job but we weren't home to do it, we thank you.

In this instance, words should not be written for they can never do you true justice and, believe me, if cops know anything, it's true justice (since we see so little of it, we know when it's right in front of us).

You've fixed our socks, picked up our uniforms from the cleaners, forgiven us for the boot polish on the carpet (eventually) and somehow, somewhere deep inside, you found a way to respect what we chose to do for a living.

You overlooked our hours (pending) you dealt with never taking that Caribbean cruise (still pending) and you explained to our kids, because we weren't there to tell them, that we weren't there *because* we loved them.

This wonderful nation has come a long way, but we've got a long, long way yet to go. When you can walk down the street, any street, at any time of day or night and not fear for a family member, we'll be on our way. When we finally begin to see people, and not skin colors, we'll really be on our way. When we begin to respect each other, regardless of our occupations or IRA's, we'll be on our way. When we try to help up a stumbling co-worker and not step on their back to get closer to a top office, we'll be on our way. When laws are written to help mankind, and not a select powerful few with hidden (political) motivators, we'll be on our way. To make it simple, when we, all of us, begin, and then live, to care about each other, then we'll be there.

We probably won't see it our lifetimes but, just maybe, our efforts, if we all start now, will protect our children from what we've experienced so often that it's now become expected every time we watch the evening news from the safety of our homes.

Until that day, my brothers and sisters will continue to clean up the mess, to respond to every call, to show you the professionalism we've tried so hard to show you every single day. If I could plead but one thing from you, it would be this.

When the media portrays a tarnished badge, you can listen to the story, Lord knows we will too, but please don't place us all in his/her shoes. The story of a fallen badge makes you sad, but it makes us sick.

Remember, behind that tarnished badge, the brilliantly shined badges that you see every day are still polished by hand, with pride, every night, for each and every one of you, and especially, for our children of tomorrow.

General Request To The American Public
Attention All Cars!

I have truly enjoyed putting my personal thoughts and experiences to paper. For those of you that had the ability to hang on this far, your endurance is admirable and I would get even more joy hearing from you.

I have listed but a few of my comments and experiences, yet you, the one's we serve, or those whom are serving us now or will serve us someday, have experienced far more. Please send your comments, letters, law enforcement contacts (good and bad, civilian or police), on and on, to:

D.W.Driver
Fife918@aol.com

A SHORT BIOGRAPHY OF THE AUTHOR

Douglas William (D.W.) Driver has been a police officer for fourteen years, as of 1998. He began his career as a reserve deputy sheriff at the Cherokee County, Oklahoma Sheriff's Department, while attending collegiate classes. Just past the age of 21 (and short of the degree he still wishes he possessed), Doug applied for and was accepted at the Northeastern Oklahoma State University Police Department, in Tahlequah, Oklahoma. Doug moved to Tahlequah from Houston Texas, where he called the residence of his grandparents home, becoming a resident of Oklahoma in an attempt to avoid out-of-state tuition fees, as well as gleefully saying goodbye to the traffic and humidity.

After six years as a campus police officer, like all other officers, he was accustomed to part time jobs and he joined a Northeastern Oklahoma grocery food chain, namely Reasor's (now Reasor's Food Warehouse), where his innocent, youthful appearance aided him well. He quickly became well known in the Tahlequah area and he was requested, by management, to venture about 70 miles away to a community about five minutes north of Tulsa, OK.

It was in this small community, of about 12,000 at the time, namely Owasso, that he really began to make a difference. He would routinely arrest between 5-8 people in an eight hour shift, travel back to Tahlequah, and do it again on his last day off. His ever devoted wife, Kelli, was ironically born and raised in Owasso and it was no time, while being a real pain in the side to the local Owasso police force, that Doug began to develop a relationship with the members of Owasso's finest. As politics began to weigh its toll on being a campus policeman, that is if you wanted to enforce the law yet stay out of a dean's office (a civilian), he applied for and was accepted as an Owasso police officer.

Within two moths of joining the Owasso force, Doug had already established two statistical records, specifically being the most citations and the most arrests, in a single month, both still unsurpassed today. He began to treat the two miles of highway, that was within his jurisdiction, as his own, and he took it extremely personal. He would, for the following years, begin to make a name for himself by his unrelenting pursuit of drunk driving offenders, particularly on "his" part of the highway. It didn't take long before he won his first "official award," by the Oklahoma Highway Safety Office, for DUI safety enforcement.

With one award, the others followed. First, and still a treasure beyond words today, was being awarded the first (annual) Owasso Police Officer of the Year. The following year, he was recognized as the Tulsa Metropolitan Police Officer of the Year, in addition to numerous local awards, including, Grand Cordon Medals, Good Conduct Medals, Citations, Commendations and DUI Enforcement awards. It was during this period of time, that the public admonition grew, that Doug became affiliated with Mothers Against Drunk Drivers, the Indian Nation Council of Governments (Hi Margaret), the Victims Impact Panel and locally, the Owasso Early Intervention Program.

In 1997, Doug was honored as the First Owasso Samaritan Police Officer of the year and, the most prestigious award in the State of Oklahoma for DUI enforcement, the Don Byerly award, named in behalf of a Tulsa Police Officer killed by a drunk driver, was presented to Officer Driver.

The year 1997 was a big one for Doug, for despite the awards previously mentioned, he became the first officer (of 72) in the United States to obtain his National Credentials as a Law Enforcement Professional, complete with a pinning ceremony in our Nation's Capitol, hosted by United States Attorney General Janet Reno. That was followed by a Governor's Commendation, Citations from the State House of Representatives and the United States Senate, including personal time with his own State Senator, the Honorable Jim Inhofe. The other Oklahoma State Senator, the Honorable Don Nichols, though out of the area at the time, made it a point to offer his best, as well. The media coverage, though very complimentary, was constant.

"If I can ever truly make a difference, yet once more in my uniformed career, that's all I'll ever want, and that's plenty to keep me polishing the badge."

~ DOUGLAS WILLIAM "D.W." DRIVER

ACCOMPLISHMENTS

1994- State of Oklahoma Municipal DUI Safety Award.
1995- (First) Owasso Police Officer Of The Year.
1996- Tulsa Metropolitan Police Officer Of The Year.
1997- (First) Owasso Samaritan Police Officer Of The Year.
1997- Don Byerely DUI Enforcement Award.
1997- (First Group Of 72 Law Enforcement Officers In The United States) Nationally Credentialized Law Enforcement Professional (Memorial Services, Washington, D.C.).
1999- United States Jaycees Outstanding Young Oklahoman in Law Enforcement.
Four (4) Grand Cordon Awards.
Three (3) Unit Citations.
Advanced Law Enforcement Certificate (State Of Oklahoma).
Good Conduct Medals (Every Year).
Three (3) Exceptional Service Medal(s).
Commendation / Excellence; Letters Of...(17).
Commendation(s)-2; Oklahoma Governor: Honorable Frank Keating.
Citation(s)-2; Oklahoma State House Of Representatives.
Commendation; United States Senate.
Founding Panelist; Early Intervention Program.
Member/Speaker; Mothers Against Drunk Drivers.
Member; INCOG / Oklahoma Highway Safety Administration/ National Highway Traffic Safety Administration
Nationally Accredited Instructor; SFST/DUI Detection.

Printed in the United States
30831LVS00001B/152

9 781591 294238